COLLABORATION EFFECT ON PROFIT

Overcoming Founder's Syndrome to Achieve Sustainable Success

By J. David Harper, Jr., and Russell H. Clemmer, IV

With Sean M. Lyden

DEDICATIONS

David Harper

To my wife, Anne.

Our twelve grandchildren—Gavin, Caleb, Avery, Allie, Hobie, Johnny, Caroline, Beau, Will, Campbell, Park, and Sadie—two sons, David and Daniel; our daughter, Lauren; son-in-law, Russ; and daughters-in-law, Becca and Laurie; all call her Annie!

She is the ultimate life-giver to everyone she meets!

Russ Clemmer

To my wife, Lauren, who shows me the Way.

Sean Lyden

To my wife, Jennifer. My coach. My cheerleader. And the most ardent believer in me when I lose faith in myself.

PREFACE

By Russ Clemmer

The subtitle of our book is *"Overcoming Founder's Syndrome to Achieve Sustainable Success."*

Why?

Let's break it down.

"Overcoming" can be a complicated word. What's involved?

Continuous action. It's not about a single event. It's about an ongoing battle against an enemy. And there's no definitive end to the "overcoming" unless you're the one who surrenders. You must stay vigilant and keep fighting.

So, what's the enemy you're overcoming?

Founder's Syndrome, which management consultant Marcus Coetze defines as a condition that "occurs when a strong-minded founder, who battled against odds to build an organization, ends up becoming its biggest constraint to growth… **Those who suffer from [Founder's Syndrome] are**

reluctant to share their power and devolve responsibilities to others in their organizations."

(See "Founder's Syndrome Undermines the Legacy of Strong Leaders" by Marcus Coetze at https://www.marcuscoetzee. com/founders-syndrome-undermines-the-legacy-of-strong-leaders/)

In short, Founder's Syndrome stifles collaboration—and growth.

Yet, here's the harsh reality: As founders and leaders, we *all* suffer from Founder's Syndrome to one degree or another. It's part of the human condition. But what can we do about it? How can we minimize its effect on our lives?

We wrote this book to tackle these questions and offer you a powerful vision of what your business, life, and legacy can look like if, day in and day out, you remain committed to "Overcoming Founder's Syndrome."

Strengthening Your Defenses

Now, we believe the root causes of Founder's Syndrome are found in **eight universal vices** that you must continually battle to "**Achieve Sustainable Success**"—the second half of the book's subtitle.

But what, exactly, does that phrase mean?

Let's start with the word "**Sustainable**."

That's because success tends to be fleeting. You get a taste of it. Things start trending in the right direction. But then the vices like Egotism, Distraction, and Greed begin to manifest in your leadership style and within your team. The next thing you know, full-blown Founder's Syndrome overwhelms you, choking off your company's growth.

So, how do you fight off the effects of Founder's Syndrome to "Achieve Sustainable Success"?

That's what you'll learn in this book.

First, we'll show you how to strengthen your **leadership character** by practicing **The Great 8 Virtues**. These virtues are the antidote to the vices that cause Founder's Syndrome.

Second, you'll learn how to instill The Great 8 Virtues throughout your company—to build and nurture a **healthy culture** where large-scale collaboration can flourish.

Finally, we'll introduce **The 3 Wins**—a powerful framework for aligning your company's financial incentives with the interests of all stakeholders to produce consistently **exceptional financial performance**.

Building Your Legacy

So, get ready! You're about to discover The Great 8 Virtues and The 3 Wins Framework. When you apply these two transformative concepts to your business and life, you'll inspire a level of collaboration among your team, customers, partners, and other stakeholders that you never imagined possible.

Everyone rowing together. In the same direction. Toward a common purpose.

That's the **Collaboration Effect on Profit (CEOP)** in action. When you unleash the CEOP, you'll build unstoppable momentum to win in any market, no matter the challenges ahead.

In other words, the CEOP is the energy that makes "Sustainable Success" a reality for any founder and leader willing to do the work—and never stop "overcoming."

Then, when you're ready to move on to the next chapter of your life, you will have built a company—with the character, culture, and financial performance—that sets up the next-generation leaders for sustainable success.

And you will have also built an enduring financial and family legacy that will impact the world for generations to come.

So, let today, by picking up this book, mark the start of your journey to *finally* create the future you've always dreamed about but couldn't see how to get there...until now.

CONTENTS

THE GREAT 8

FEAR
COURAGE
TERRITORIALISM
EGOTISM
PEACEMAKING
HUMILITY
DISHONESTY
BUSYNESS
INTEGRITY
EMPATHY
ACCEPTANCE
ATTENTIVENESS
ANGER
DISTRACTION
ACCOUNTABILITY
GREED

COLLABORATION EFFECT ON PROFIT

SHAREHOLDER
COMPANY
THE
3 WINS
KEY LEADER

LEGACY

INTRODUCTION:
PURSUING FULL ALIGNMENT

"If you could get all the people in an organization rowing in the same direction, you could dominate any industry, in any market, against any competition, at any time."
- Patrick Lencioni, The Five Dysfunctions of a Team: A Leadership Fable

By David Harper

This book has been many years in the making.

I began my entrepreneurial career in 1978 as a solo financial advisor. But it wasn't until 2000 that my late business partner, Bill Straub, and I formally launched (what is now) Legacy Advisory Partners, a financial services firm specializing in executive benefits.

Like many of you, we had numerous struggles—lack of alignment, no clear mission, loose budgeting and forecasting, poor organizational structure, and difficulty with accountability.

But we had reasonable financial success, and that success masked our struggles. I had blind spots to these issues—*my* issues—primarily because I was suffering from Founder's Syndrome.

The Problem: Founder's Syndrome (Chapters 1-2)

Founders often start working out of their pickup truck, basement, or garage. And then, sales grow, and several people get hired, and the company reaches a point where you say, "I have a real business!"

But at this stage, you're still wearing multiple hats and spinning most of the plates, making your work-life balance out of whack.

That's when Founder's Syndrome kicks in.

Founder's Syndrome is a phenomenon where the founder refuses to change gears despite clear evidence that the habits that got them to initial success—"shooting from the hip," closing all the sales, making all the decisions—have become liabilities stunting their company's growth.

You can tell a founder who is afflicted by it because they maintain excessive control and influence over the business, often to its detriment. Since they're unwilling to "let go," they tend to stifle collaboration, not promote it. As a result, they struggle with attracting, developing, and retaining the strong leaders they need to put their company on a path to sustainable success.

But Founder's Syndrome does not only apply to the original founder of an organization. It can also afflict *anyone* in leadership who's "holding on too tight"—who says, "I built this thing (this department, division, committee), and no one is taking it away from me!"

We wrote this book because we believe that every one of us as leaders suffers from Founder's Syndrome to some degree. And, if we don't become aware of its impact on our lives and businesses, we'll continue down a path of self-sabotage, feeling powerless to change course.

Now, it's one thing to admit you struggle with Founder's Syndrome. But what can you do about it? How can you fight it off?

We found the answer in The Great 8 Virtues.

The Solution: The Great 8 Virtues (Chapters 3-10)

From 2000-2010, our company experienced dysfunction because I struggled with Founder's Syndrome but was completely unaware of it. Relationships were strained, and confidence was low.

But around 2010, Bill and I rediscovered the dynamite of the Bible in Matthew 5—The Beatitudes. And our view of everything radically changed—in our lives, business, families, and relationships.

The Beatitudes are the opening to Jesus's "Sermon on the Mount," where he outlines eight timeless principles for thinking about and living out our role in "the Kingdom of God" in today's world.

We challenged ourselves: "What would our business look like if we built it on these eight principles?"

That's when we began developing The Great 8 for our company—eight *virtues* and their corresponding *vices* based on the Beatitudes:

Beatitude #1 = Virtue #1: Humility vs. Egotism

"Blessed are the poor in spirit, for theirs is the kingdom of heaven."

~ Matt. 5:3

Beatitude #2 = Virtue #2: Epathy vs. Busyness

"Blessed are those who mourn, for they will be comforted."

~ Matt. 5:4

Beatitude #3 = Virtue #3: Attentiveness vs. Distraction

"Blessed are the meek, for they will inherit the earth."

~ Matt. 5:5

Beatitude #4 = Virtue #4: Accountability vs. Greed

"Blessed are those who hunger and thirst for righteousness, for they will be filled."

~ Matt. 5:6

Beatitude #5 = Virtue #5: Acceptance vs. Anger

"Blessed are the merciful, for they will be shown mercy."

~ Matt. 5:7

Beatitude #6 = Virtue #6: Integrity vs. Dishonesty

"Blessed are the pure in heart, for they will see God."

~ Matt. 5:8

Beatitude #7 = Virtue #7: Peacemaking vs. Territorialism

"Blessed are the peacemakers, for they will be called children of God."

~ Matt. 5:9

Beatitude #8 = Virtue #8: Courage vs. Fear

"Blessed are those who are persecuted because of righteousness, for theirs is the kingdom of heaven."

~ Matt. 5:10

We came to realize that the vices (Egotism, Busyness, Distraction, Greed, etc.) were root causes of Founder's Syndrome. But if we committed to practicing The Great 8 Virtues and instilling them into our team, we could attack Founder's Syndrome at its source—the vices.

That's when the hard work began. But it was well worth it.

For example:

- We saw strategic discussions move from fear-based to outcome-focused, where each team member had their "full say" and felt safe to argue their case fully.

- We saw our workday move from chaotic Busyness to a sharper focus on our Most Important Tasks (MITs).

- We saw team conflict move from passive-aggressive (where people would "get their feelings hurt" and bury it) to immediate and respectful resolution.

- We saw roles and responsibilities move from silos and competition to high levels of collaboration.

But when Bill passed away in 2013, I found myself slipping into the vices again, allowing Founder's Syndrome to creep back in. I knew we needed a clear business succession plan but kept putting it off. I held our numbers close to the vest, refusing to be transparent with our team. I still operated "at the center of the circle" in the business with no delegation plan and no plan to replicate myself. And the company had no path to succeed to the next generation of leadership.

During my struggle with running Legacy after Bill, our team and I committed to getting the virtues so ingrained in us that it would become our company's DNA. So, I began putting The Great 8 Virtues into writing. This process of reflection renewed my conviction to fight off Founder's Syndrome and start "letting go" to build a more dynamic culture of collaboration.

The result of my time "in the wilderness" is the book I published in 2015–*The Great 8: A New Paradigm for Leadership*.

In 2016, we began expanding upon that book by writing articles about The Great 8 for our email newsletter. These articles sparked numerous conversations—and engagements—with founders who asked us to help them adopt The Great 8 in their companies.

The Confusion: How do Virtues Relate to Financial Services? (Chapter 11)

Shortly after launching our newsletter, a long-time client gave us feedback that would ultimately inspire us to write this book.

He said he understood the importance of the virtues in building a healthy culture but couldn't understand why *we* were discussing them. Legacy is a financial services company. Did something change? Are we now a leadership development and consulting company?

After all, what do virtues have to do with financial services?

We could understand the confusion. But, in our minds, The Great 8 Virtues have *everything* to do with financial services and our client's long-term success.

That's because financial solutions by themselves are not enough. Smart financial strategies—such as long-term incentive plans and non-qualified deferred compensation plans—yield the best outcomes in companies that nurture a high-trust, virtuous culture where the spirit of collaboration can flourish.

Without the Great 8 Virtues guiding the team, even the most well-intentioned performance incentives may inadvertently encourage negative behaviors—such as Greed, Territorialism, and Egotism.

We became convinced that God's design for successful businesses includes a laser focus on promoting collaborative behaviors around a common purpose. We also realized how much of a contrast this perspective is to how most businesses are run. In most "successful" companies, you often see so much collateral damage:

- Families suffer from neglect—too much attention given to the business, with nothing left for the home front.

- Employees burn out.

- Pursuing the "big check" at the end of the rainbow becomes all important, no matter the cost to health and relationships.

- Employees feel pressured to make ethical compromises, trying to achieve unrealistic numbers.

Ultimately, we arrived at the belief that The Great 8 is the moral compass every company needs to avoid the collateral damage prevalent in mainstream "greed-based" capitalism.

The Connection: The 3 Wins Framework (Chapters 12-15)

But how do you translate virtuous character and culture into real-world financial success?

Answering that question led us to discover The 3 Wins in 2018.

The 3 Wins is a framework that aligns the power of The Great 8 Virtues—to strengthen **character** and transform **culture**—with the interests and incentives that drive stellar **financial performance.**

This framework takes a holistic and balanced approach to financial decision-making to create complete alignment—where all three parties "win" simultaneously.

1. **The shareholders win...**by growing a sustainably profitable business that produces the means they need to build an impactful financial legacy for their families for future generations.

2. **The company wins...**by nurturing "the golden goose"–the business–to strengthen its short- and long-term growth and marketability prospects.

3. **The key leaders win...**by creating an environment where they feel fulfilled in their career path and confident they can build a financial legacy for their families.

Balance is the key that unlocks the value of The 3 Wins. Otherwise, if one party wins, but one or two of the others do not, *everyone* ultimately loses.

When you combine **The 3 Wins (financial performance)** with **The Great 8 Virtues (character and culture)**, you lay the foundation for sustainable and profitable growth that avoids the typical collateral damage of success from the traditional approach to business. In so many cases, people become victims of their success in a way that causes marriages and families to suffer because the business demands too much. And employees feel used and burned out.

But The 3 Wins Framework guides you in setting bold financial targets balanced with your team's capacity to achieve those goals. And The Great 8 Virtues help you nurture a high-trust culture where your team feels the psychological safety to collaborate at the highest level.

Combine The 3 Wins with The Great 8, and that's when the magic happens.

The Outcome: The Collaboration Effect on Profit (Chapter 16)

When you build an environment where ownership, leadership, and rank-and-file employees all work together in their optimal roles toward a common purpose, you create a force multiplier to achieve breakthrough—and sustainable—growth.

That's the Collaboration Effect on Profit (CEOP).

At this point, the founder is no longer a constraint on the company. Instead, they're laser-focused on building, guiding, and empowering their team to produce financial results they could never achieve on their own.

T3W x TG8 = CEOP

We think about the relationship between The 3 Wins and The Great 8 with this formula:

The 3 Wins X The Great 8 = the Collaboration Effect on Profit

Following this formula positions the business to:

- Break through barriers to sustainable growth
- Become significantly more valuable
- Continue to thrive under next-generation ownership, whatever that may be—sale to a third party, employee stock ownership plan (ESOP), internal sale to the management team, or transfer to family members.

As Patrick Lencioni writes in *The Five Dysfunctions of a Team: A Leadership Fable,* "If you could get all the people in an organization rowing in the same direction, you could dominate any industry, in any market, against any competition, at any time."

When you align character, culture, and financial performance to get everyone "rowing in the same direction," you'll unleash the CEOP–to put your company in the best position to win in any market under any conditions.

Profit = Advantage

A quick side note about profit…When we use the word "profit" in the context of CEOP, we refer to more than just money. Mark 8:36 says, "For what shall a man profit if he gains the whole world and loses his soul?" The Greek word for profit in this verse is *opheleo*, which means "advantage."

So, when we say we want to create the Collaboration Effect on Profit, we mean that we want to create an *advantage* for all stakeholders–the shareholders, the company, key leaders, all employees, customers, investors, and vendors, along with all their families.

In other words, collaboration creates an advantage–an overwhelming one for all participants.

The Legacy: Passing the Baton to the Next Generation

Once you've aligned The Great 8 Virtues and The 3 Wins to unleash the CEOP, you've created the ideal conditions for passing the baton of your business to the next-generation leaders.

How do we know?

We've lived it at Legacy Advisory Partners.

When my son-in-law, Russ Clemmer, joined our team in 2014, we had already been putting The Great 8 Virtues into place. But Russ began to challenge me to get the principles of success, numbers, and methods out of my head and into systems and processes so I could start "getting out of the center of the circle" of the business.

Russ' push to systematize our business led to us discovering what would eventually become The 3 Wins Framework. Over time, we developed and formalized our internal approach to The 3 Wins to share it with our clients. And now, with this book, we're sharing it with you—as you prepare your business, your key leaders, and yourself for the next chapter in your company's story.

On November 1, 2023, we celebrated the "passing of the baton" at Legacy as Russ and another long-time colleague, Marc Walker, took the reins, leading our company forward beyond me.

We've come a long way in nearly 25 years.

Founder's Syndrome held me—and the company—back for far too long. But the discoveries of The Great 8 Virtues and, then, The 3 Wins Framework gave us the tools to fight off Founder's Syndrome, break through our barriers to growth, and create a path to sustainable success for our next-generation leaders.

We hope and pray that the ideas in this book will have a similar life-changing impact on you and your team as they have had on us.

The Next Step: How to Read This Book

How can you get the most out of this book? We recommend taking the following approach:

Step 1: Read.

Read straight through the first time to familiarize yourself with The Great 8 Virtues and The 3 Wins.

Step 2: Return.

Return to "Chapter 16: Putting It All Together: Unleashing the Collaboration Effect on Profit in Your Business—and Your Life." Follow the six steps to begin transforming yourself and your company.

Step 3: Revisit.

Revisit the book periodically. The idea here is that the CEOP is not a Set-It-and-Forget-It approach to business and personal growth. It requires discipline, vigilance, and a commitment to continuous application and improvement.

Ready to take the next step toward transforming your life and business?

Let's get started!

PART 1:
KNOW THY ENEMY

CHAPTER 1:
FOUNDER'S SYNDROME: THE WARNING SIGNS

"No man will make a great leader who wants to do it all himself or get all the credit for doing it."
- Andrew Carnegie

He had the textbook case of Founder's Syndrome.

He led "from the center of the circle"—where all critical actions and decision-making had to run through him. His overbearing and abrasive leadership style created a chaotic, abusive, and drama-filled work environment. And he shut down negative feedback and criticism, convinced of the correctness of his actions, even when he was wrong.

As a result, key leaders and rank-and-file employees were rowing in different directions, bringing the company to a crisis point.

Ultimately, Founder's Syndrome led to him being ousted from the organization he built.

But after an 11-year exile from Apple Inc., co-founder Steve Jobs rejoined the company a changed man. Somehow, he learned how to fight off Founder's Syndrome and reemerged to become one of the most transformative entrepreneurs in history.

When Your Strengths Become Liabilities

This story begins in 1976 when Jobs, with Steve Wozniak and Ronald Wayne, founded Apple Inc. Jobs was the quintessential charismatic leader, driving his team with his sheer will to build a world-changing company from scratch. He was instrumental in developing the Apple I and Apple II computers, which helped lay the foundation for the personal computer revolution.

But like many entrepreneurs, Jobs was afflicted by Founder's Syndrome, where the traits that helped him build Apple into a household brand—his demanding management style, force-of-nature personality, and fierce competitiveness— also led to his dismissal from the company.

In other words, his strengths became liabilities, hindering Apple from entering its next growth phase.

The tipping point arrived when the Lisa and Macintosh computers, Jobs' pet projects, didn't perform as expected in the market. This triggered a power struggle between Jobs and then-CEO John Sculley over the company's direction.

Jobs wanted to focus on the Macintosh, which he saw as the future of computing. He was convinced that its graphical user interface would make computing accessible to the masses. But Sculley and other board members believed that the Macintosh was too expensive and wanted to focus on the

Apple II, a significant revenue generator for the company at the time.

The board sided with Sculley, and Jobs was removed from his role leading the Macintosh division. He was offered a position that was described as ceremonial—a chairman's position with no operational duties.

Feeling sidelined, Jobs resigned from Apple in September 1985.

Although history would prove Jobs was correct about the Macintosh, his ego and stubbornness—hallmarks of Founder's Syndrome—caused him to lose the influence he needed to win over the board to his perspective.

The Transformation

The following 11 years marked a time of reflection, growth, and change for Jobs. During his exile from Apple, Jobs founded NeXT, a computer platform company, and bought Pixar, the now-famous animation company on the verge of going out of business at the time.

Meanwhile, Apple was struggling in the mid-1990s. It needed a fresh direction and a creative spark. And, in a twist of fate, Apple acquired NeXT in December 1996, bringing Jobs back into the fold.

Jobs initially returned in an advisory role. But he soon accepted an executive position as interim CEO in September 1997. The "interim" tag was dropped in 2000, and he remained CEO until his resignation for health reasons in August 2011.

While he was still a demanding leader, something clearly changed in him.

Jobs moved out of "the center of the circle" of the business, discovering the importance of collaboration and harnessing the strengths of a team. He surrounded himself with talented executives like Tim Cook (now Apple's CEO) and Jony Ive, entrusting them with significant responsibilities.

Though still intensely involved in product development, Jobs eased off his overbearing leadership style, allowing others to thrive in their roles and fostering a more dynamic, innovative environment.

And he created a new culture of excellence that embraced open communication and feedback as a path to learning and success, a departure from the fear-driven culture of his early leadership.

Now, instead of stoking infighting, strife, and chaos, Jobs had gotten everyone at Apple rowing in the same direction.

And the rest is history. Apple launched a series of groundbreaking products: the iMac, iPod, iPhone, and iPad. Each of these disrupted their respective markets and propelled Apple to become one of the most valuable companies in the world.

Lessons in Exile

The big takeaway from Steve Jobs' story is that Founder's Syndrome isn't permanent. You don't have to resign to it, thinking, "Well, that's just who I am."

No. You can overcome Founder's Syndrome. And you can grow into becoming the leader your company needs to get to the next level.

Consider these six lessons Jobs learned in exile that helped him fight off Founder's Syndrome and become the CEO who would take Apple to unprecedented heights:

1. **Humility:** Being ousted from Apple was a humbling experience for Jobs. This period forced him to reflect on his actions and leadership style, which he admitted in later interviews was necessary for him to mature as a leader.

2. **Delegation:** Jobs learned to delegate and trust his team more, partially out of necessity. When he was running both NeXT and Pixar, he simply couldn't manage everything. At Apple, he empowered executives like Tim Cook and Jony Ive to take on major responsibilities.

3. **Collaboration:** Jobs never completely lost his demanding nature, but he learned to temper it with more respect for others. His experience at Pixar, where a creative and collaborative culture was essential, likely influenced this change.

4. **Perspective:** During his time away, Jobs had the chance to see Apple from the outside, and it became clear that the company needed to be bigger than just one person. When he returned, he worked on creating an institutional culture that could survive without him.

5. **Succession:** While Jobs was notorious for his hands-on approach, he also began to prepare for a future Apple without him. He set up Apple University to train executives in 'the Apple way' of doing things and started grooming Tim Cook, his eventual successor, years before his death.

6. **Adaptability:** Jobs' wilderness period was filled with failures (like the initial struggles of NeXT and Pixar) and successes. These experiences likely helped him develop resilience and adaptability—traits that were crucial when he returned to Apple, which was on the brink of bankruptcy.

10 Symptoms of Founder's Syndrome

Founder's Syndrome is a psychological condition where the founder resists change despite clear evidence that the habits that got them to initial success—"shooting from the hip," closing all the sales, making all the decisions—have become liabilities stunting their company's growth.

You can tell a founder who is afflicted by it because they maintain excessive control and influence over the business, often to its detriment.

But you don't have to be the original founder to succumb to Founder's Syndrome. In fact, even second-, third, and later-generation CEOs are also vulnerable to it. That's because whichever generation you are, the issue is the same: Control vs. collaboration. Too much control will stifle collaboration and choke off growth.

So, how can you assess your risk of Founder's Syndrome? Look for these 10 symptoms:

1. **Centralization of decision-making:** Do you dominate decision-making processes and resist delegation of authority, leading to bottlenecks and inefficiencies?

2. **Lack of succession planning:** Do you resist the idea of a successor, creating a leadership vacuum or crisis when you can no longer lead?

3. **Micromanagement:** Are you overly involved in day-to-day operations, undermining the authority of other leaders or managers?

4. **Lack of diverse thinking:** Do you surround yourself with those who are too timid to challenge your decisions?

5. **Poor financial management:** Do you exert too much control over the organization's finances, potentially making unsound decisions or failing to plan for the future adequately?

6. **Inability to delegate:** Do you struggle to trust others with important tasks, leading to burnout and an overworked team?

7. **Lack of organizational structure:** Have you avoided establishing clear roles, responsibilities, and reporting structures, leading to confusion and inefficiency within the company?

8. **Inability to scale:** Do you struggle to adapt the organization's processes and strategies to

accommodate growth, leading to operational challenges and missed opportunities?

9. **Fear of losing control:** Are you resistant to outside investors, partners, or board members who could provide valuable guidance or resources due to a fear of losing control or influence over the organization?

10.**Neglecting work-life balance:** Are you so committed to the business that you neglect your personal life, health, or well-being, which can lead to burnout and reduced effectiveness?

Do you experience any of these symptoms? Which ones strike closest to home?

As with any affliction, the starting point to overcoming Founder's Syndrome is to admit you're dealing with it. Then, the next step is to treat the root causes, not the symptoms.

How do you uncover the root causes of *your* specific case of Founder's Syndrome?

Take the Founder's Syndrome Root Cause Survey in Chapter 2.

CHAPTER 2:
THE VICES: GETTING AT THE ROOTS OF FOUNDER'S SYNDROME

"Search others for their virtues, thyself for thy vices."
- Benjamin Franklin

D o you feel trapped inside your business, where little happens until *you* make the decisions?

Do you put off taking vacations because you can't trust your team to keep the business running while you're away?

Are you too overwhelmed to dedicate enough time to developing your key leaders?

These are just a few symptoms of Founder's Syndrome, as detailed in the previous chapter. But if you're afflicted by it, what can you do? How can you fight it?

The Root Causes: 8 Vices

The starting point for overcoming Founder's Syndrome is to identify its root causes—these eight universal vices that impact every entrepreneur and their team to varying degrees:

Vice #1: Egotism

The *Oxford English Dictionary* defines Egotism as "the excessive practice of thinking and talking about oneself due to an inflated sense of self-worth." Unchecked, Egotism hinders your ability to trust and empower your team, stifles ambitious thinking, and discourages hiring talented individuals to bring your dreams to life.

Vice #2: Busyness

Busyness is not the same thing as "being busy." But when your work consumes you, "busy" crosses the line to Busyness, a vice that strains your relationships, diminishes productivity, and causes team burnout.

Vice #3: Distraction

Distraction is taking your eye off the proverbial ball—your mission, team, and priorities. And that's when you become most prone to making costly mistakes. You divert your attention from important tasks and goals to engage in trivial or sometimes harmful activities, undermining your productivity, relationships, and personal development.

Vice #4: Greed

Greed is the selfish pursuit of money, pleasure, and power at the expense of others' interests. These pursuits are not inherently wrong, but when approached with improper motives, they become destructive, leaving you unsatisfied and empty.

Vice #5: Anger

Anger arises when obstacles prevent you from achieving your desires. Although occasional expressions of anger are justified (as in "righteous indignation"), uncontrolled Anger is harmful. It deteriorates trust, hampers team performance, and may push your most talented employees to seek opportunities elsewhere.

Vice #6: Dishonesty

Dishonesty involves intentionally lying or withholding truth for personal gain or self-preservation. Such deception can lead to the breakdown of trust and fairness in relationships. When Dishonesty influences your decisions, you become divided, living a double life: one aligned with truth and the other struggling to reconcile truth with your actions.

Vice #7: Territorialism

Territorialism is about scarcity—fear of loss. It causes people to get defensive and protect their turf at all costs. It sees business as a zero-sum game: "For me to win, I must make sure you lose." This vice creates a divisive atmosphere and promotes unproductive competition.

Vice #8: Fear

Fear is a natural emotion that signals potential threats. However, when Fear becomes excessive or unfounded, it becomes a destructive vice. It narrows your perspective, highlighting only the worst-case scenarios and limiting your ability to consider all options to make well-informed decisions.

The Founder's Syndrome Root Cause Survey

How prevalent is Founder's Syndrome in your leadership style? What vices–or root causes–affect your decision-making and team interactions?

Take this survey to uncover your vulnerabilities. Below are 40 questions related to the eight vices that can contribute to Founder's Syndrome. Respond to each using a 1-5 scale (1 = Strongly Disagree, 2 = Disagree, 3 = Neutral, 4 = Agree, and 5 = Strongly Agree).

Afterward, rank these vices based on your highest to lowest scores to identify the most likely root causes of your case of Founder's Syndrome.

Here are the questions:

Vice #1: Egotism

1. I occasionally take back responsibilities I've delegated to "make sure they're done right."
2. I don't trust my team to perform critical tasks without my direct involvement.
3. I am the only one who can fix the company's problems.
4. The company can't succeed without me.
5. I tend to discount negative feedback.

Egotism Score:

Vice #2: Busyness

1. I seldom take vacations or time off because the company will stumble in my absence. _____

2. Working excessively long hours is common for me. _____

3. I struggle to find enough time to develop my team. _____

4. I struggle with saying No to new "opportunities." _____

5. My relationships at home/ my personal life are unraveling. _____

Busyness Score: _____

Vice #3: Distraction

1. I struggle with *consistent* follow-through on my commitments. _____

2. I've been known to change the company's strategy "on a whim." _____

3. I can get easily sidetracked by new ideas. _____

4. I find myself making too many careless errors. _____

5. My personal problems tend to affect my work. _____

Distraction Score: _____

Vice #4: Greed

1. I've tolerated toxic behavior from top-performing leaders._____

2. I've felt resentful about "paying out too much" in incentives/ bonuses to employees._____

3. I've allowed a client's size to determine whether I tolerate their abuse toward my employees._____

4. I've felt the urge to change a sales rep's compensation plan when they're "earning too much."_____

5. I don't need accountability to run my business effectively._____

Greed Score: _____

Vice #5: Anger

1. I tend to be the last person in the company to hear "bad news"—often when it's too late._____

2. I've been known to come across to others as "unapproachable."_____

3. I struggle with keeping my composure in front of my team when I "have a bad day."_____

4. I've lashed out at employees in front of their colleagues._____

5. I have difficulty seeing an employee's full potential when they struggle to live up to my expectations in their current role._____

Anger Score: _____

Vice #6: Dishonesty

1. I tend to avoid giving candid feedback. _____

2. I've exaggerated or downplayed facts to portray situations more favorably to my interests. _____

3. I've withheld important negative news from my team, customers, and/or other stakeholders to protect my own interests. _____

4. I struggle with admitting mistakes. _____

5. I've steered customers toward higher-margin offerings when a lower-cost solution would be better for their specific problem. _____

Dishonesty Score: _____

Vice #7: Territorialism

1. I occasionally find myself competing against my team in an unproductive way. _____

2. I feel threatened when others challenge my position or status in the company. _____

3. I establish boundaries that deter others from contributing to my areas of responsibility. _____

4. I am resistant to sharing power or control over significant decisions. _____

5. I believe that "making peace" with someone means to "let things go" instead of confronting the issue (and the person) head-on. _____

Territorialism Score: _____

Vice #8: Fear

1. I'm known to be a "perfectionist."

2. I sometimes justify Fear by saying, "I'm just being prudent."

3. I tend to put off important decisions longer than I should.

4. I have allowed the fear of failure to hold me back.

5. I struggle to "think big."

Fear Score:

Total Score:

The Analysis

Now, let's look at your results. Add up all your responses to calculate your total score. Refer to this guide to identify where you fit:

40-80: Code Green–Healthy Balance: You've struck a productive balance between personal control and team performance. But remain alert. Market conditions and business dynamics can change, increasing your susceptibility to Founder's Syndrome.

81-120: Code Yellow–Mild Symptoms: There are some indications of Founder's Syndrome, but it hasn't significantly impacted your business yet.

121-160: Code Orange–Moderate to Severe Condition: Founder's Syndrome is stunting your company's growth.

161-200: Code Red–Critical Condition: Founder's Syndrome is causing significant harm to you and your company.

Ranking the Root Causes

Which root causes–or vices–expose you most to Founder's Syndrome?

Determine this by ranking your individual Vice Scores from 1-8, starting from the highest to the lowest:

1. _____

2. _____

3. _____

4. _____

5. _____

6. _____

7. _____

8. _____

Reflect on your results. What insights have you gained from this exercise?

Over the following eight chapters, we'll introduce each of the Great 8 Virtues that will help you attack Founder's Syndrome at its roots. You will learn how to put each virtue into practice–to fight off Founder's Syndrome, transform your culture, and set the table for achieving The 3 Wins that unleash the Collaboration Effect on Profit in your business.

Ready to go on the attack?

PART 2:
Fight Off Founder's Syndrome with The Great 8 Virtues

CHAPTER 3:
VIRTUE #1: HUMILITY VS. EGOTISM

> *"Do you wish to rise? Begin by descending. Do you plan a tower that will pierce the clouds? Lay first the foundation of humility."*
> **- St. Augustine**

Which type of leader are you—a chess master or a gardener?

The chess master vs. gardener metaphor comes from General Stanley McChrystal's *Team of Teams: New Rules of Engagement for a Complex World*. He tells the story about how he led like a chess master for most of his career. He controlled each piece on the "board" as his unit awaited his "next move."

But when McChrystal took the helm of the Joint Special Operations Command (JSOC) during the Iraq War in 2003, it didn't take long for him to realize the conventional top-down approach to decision-making wasn't working.

Why?

He and his team faced a highly adaptive and networked enemy in the form of Al Qaeda in Iraq (AQI). With its bureaucracy and hierarchical structure, JSOC initially struggled against AQI's decentralized and flexible operations, giving the enemy these advantages:

- **Faster decision-making:** AQI was able to move and adapt quickly, exploiting the slow decision-making processes inherent in bureaucratic structures. The traditional hierarchy within JSOC required decisions to move up and down the chain of command, which delayed responses to insurgent attacks.

- **Faster information sharing:** The siloed nature of JSOC at the time hindered the free flow of crucial information across different units and teams. But AQI's decentralized structure allowed for quicker information dissemination and coordinated action.

McChrystal came to recognize how his top-down "chess master" approach was failing against an enemy that operated more like a distributed network than a conventional military unit. "I had to adapt to the new reality and reshape myself, as conditions were forcing us to reshape our force. And so I stopped playing chess, and I became a gardener," McCrystal writes.

The Shift to a Gardener

To counter AQI's adaptability, McChrystal led a transformation of JSOC into a "team of teams" — a networked organization where information and decision-making authority flowed more freely among highly empowered teams. This new structure was more akin to being a "gardener" who fosters the right environment for teams to adapt quickly to new information and challenges.

The gardener puts ego aside, entrusting their teams to make critical decisions. "The move-by-move control that seemed natural to military operations proved less effective than nurturing the organization, its structure, processes, and culture to enable the subordinate components to function with 'smart autonomy,'" McCrystal writes.

Instead of micromanaging people and decisions, the gardener focuses on "nurturing the culture"—by feeding the soil, creating the optimal conditions, and pruning where necessary—to produce the best people and decisions. As McCrystal writes, "The gardener creates an environment where the plants can flourish. The work done upfront, and vigilant maintenance, allow the plants to grow individually, all at the same time."

McCrystal's transformation to gardener-style leadership significantly increased JSOC's effectiveness and was vital in diminishing AQI's capabilities in Iraq.

Chess Master = Leading From the Center of the Circle

As founders, our default mode tends to be the chess master. At Legacy, we call it "leading from the center of the circle"—where all critical actions and decision-making only run through the owner.

Now, when the business is just you and a handful of people, you can get by with being the chess master. But you can't stay like that if you want to grow the business. Otherwise, you'll be the bottleneck. Eventually, you'll need to shift from centralized control to empowered teams—from chess master to gardener.

But, to make that change, you must first confront a powerful and relentless enemy. And it's not the market. It's not your competitor. It's not anyone or anything else.

It's you—your ego. It's the vice of Egotism grabbing your neck and suffocating your company's growth potential.

Egotism Defined

What is Egotism?

The *Oxford English Dictionary* defines Egotism as "the practice of talking and thinking about oneself excessively because of an undue sense of self."

Yet, many of us will look at this definition and say, "Yeah. I can think of many people this definition pertains to, but it's not me!"

But as C.S. Lewis said, "If you think you are not conceited, it means you are very conceited indeed."

Egotism is such an insidious vice because we don't see it in ourselves until it's too late. That's when we get blindsided by sales declines, competitive pressures, and key-leader defections. If left unchecked, Egotism compels us to lead from the center of the circle, where we don't trust our teams to execute independently without our direct involvement.

This mindset creates a culture of dependency and control that stifles growth. Risk-averse employees may stay in this toxic environment to "go along to get along."

But who wants an office full of people who hate their jobs? Talented people will say, "Enough!" and leave to work for a competitor or even start a competing company themselves. Owners stuck in the ego trap will point the finger of blame at the unhappy employees who left.

They can't see how their actions led to those employees wanting to leave.

Egotism at Scale: Poor Teamwork

What happens when Egotism spreads beyond the owner to infect the entire team?

You see it in professional sports. There are countless examples of talented teams failing to live up to their hype. Each individual on those all-star teams wants to do things their way. They focus on building up their own status rather than on team success.

These "stars" hog credit for wins and deflect blame for losses. So, they struggle to work together as a single unit. As a result, they become vulnerable to losing to less talented teams that put their egos aside and support their teammates.

A culture that rewards individual status over teamwork stifles collaboration. Why?

Employees don't trust that management and their peers have their best interests in mind. So, they work against each other to protect their status and egos. They don't feel the psychological safety to be vulnerable with one another. And it's vulnerability that produces the team chemistry that marks the highest-performing companies.

Fighting Off Egotism with Humility

Egotism is at the root of chronic small thinking. It constrains owners from dreaming big about their business. And it discourages them from hiring talented people to make their vision a reality.

So how can you break the ego's grip—and break the bottleneck to your company's growth?

Start by practicing Humility, the first of The Great 8 Virtues. Humility leads to self-awareness. It produces honesty with yourself and others about your strengths and weaknesses. It empowers you to look beyond yourself and your own "wins." This way, you can recognize that, for you to win, the company and your key leaders must win, too.

That's The 3 Wins Framework in a nutshell, which we'll discuss in Part 3 of this book. You win. Your company wins. Your key leaders win. And it's Humility that makes The 3 Wins possible.

As the famous 19th-century preacher Charles H. Spurgeon said, "Humility is to make a right estimate of oneself." But practicing "to make a right estimate of oneself" must begin with you. Then, you're in the right frame of mind to create a safe environment for your team to follow your lead.

Humble owners share credit for team successes and accept responsibility for failures. This attitude is a prerequisite to a high-trust, collaborative culture. That's because team members don't have to "watch their back." They can trust that management will notice and reward their contributions.

"If certain conditions are met, and the people inside an organization feel safe among each other, they will work together to achieve things none of them could have ever achieved alone," Simon Sinek writes in *Leaders Eat Last: Why Some Teams Pull Together and Others Don't.*

Humility produces a winning team built on psychological safety and shared vulnerability. Now, each employee feels empowered to operate in their sweet spot to succeed for the company.

Humility = Confidence

Before we go further, let's address some misconceptions about Humility. It's not "Aw shucks" bashfulness. It's not self-pity. And it's not timidity (which is a form of protecting the ego from the pain of potential rejection). These mentalities are self-focused and self-preserving—they're Egotism in humble clothing.

In reality, Humility is not weakness. It's the confidence that gives us the strength to be vulnerable. It empowers us to confront the truth about ourselves, no matter how ugly that might be.

That's what makes Humility such a powerful force against Egotism. "When we remove ego, we're left with what is real," Ryan Holiday writes in *Ego is the Enemy*. "What replaces ego is humility, yes—but rock-hard humility and confidence. Whereas ego is artificial, this type of confidence can hold weight. Ego is stolen. Confidence is earned. Ego is self-anointed; its swagger is artifice."

In other words, Egotism may make us feel strong and confident at the moment, but it gives us a false sense of security. It becomes toxic to our culture, pushing others away—the same people we need to help us succeed.

Humility, on the other hand, creates an environment that attracts the talent you need to build your business into a high-performing machine.

Putting Humility into Practice

It's one thing to say, "Hey, be humble!" But how exactly do you do that?

Here are eight practical steps to apply the virtue of Humility to your life and leadership style:

1. Be self-aware about how Egotism influences your decision-making.

As C.S. Lewis writes in *Mere Christianity*, "If anyone would like to acquire humility, I can, I think, tell him the first step. The first step is to realize that one is proud."

2. Be open to self-examination.

Ask yourself, "Am I being a bottleneck to our growth? Is what I'm doing working? How do I need to adapt to improve our results?"

3. Lead by example.

Do you want your team to put their egos aside for the company's best interests? That starts at the top. When you lead with Humility, you gain the credibility you need to ask your team to follow your lead.

4. Encourage candor.

Listen to your team's concerns and honest input. Create an environment where they feel "safe" to give negative feedback without retribution.

5. Shift your leadership style from chess master to gardener.

Create a culture that produces great leaders you can trust to help you grow the business.

6. Nurture the garden; don't neglect it.

Leadership is not a set-it-and-forget-it activity. So, tend to your garden—your team. Help each individual grow and flourish. "A gardening approach to leadership is anything but passive," McCrystal writes. "The leader acts as an 'Eyes-On, Hands-Off' enabler who creates and maintains an ecosystem in which the organization operates."

7. Hear people out, even when they're making excuses or blaming others.

Everything in you will want to stop and correct them immediately. But be patient. Hear them out so that they feel understood. This way, they'll be more willing to put down their defenses and listen to your feedback and coaching.

8. Be willing to have tough conversations.

You'll need to have some heart-to-heart conversations with people. If you lay everything out for them—and they respond with openness and Humility—then coach them up. But if they refuse to listen and continue blaming others, you might need to let them go. Otherwise, they'll undermine your efforts to promote teamwork.

Humility at Scale: Role Optimization

How can you instill the virtue of Humility throughout your company?

Put a system in place where you and your key leaders review everyone's roles and giftedness. This way, you'll discover how to get everyone into their optimal role, all rowing in the same direction.

Unfortunately, good people get stuck in bad roles that don't fit them. Or they don't understand what their role should be. In either case, they may not meet expectations even when they give their best effort.

So, assess your own and your team's performance. Is everyone placed in the best position to achieve professional and personal fulfillment? If not, what adjustments can you make to bridge the gaps between their actual and optimal roles?

We call this exercise "Role Optimization." It taps into Jim Collin's bus metaphor in *Good to Great: Why Some Companies Make the Leap and Others Don't*. He says to, first, get the right people "on the bus." Then put them in "the right seats"—in other words, their optimal role.

But how do you determine "the right seats"? Use these questions as a guide:

1. What roles do we need to fill to achieve our vision?

Look at the organizational chart. Have you identified all required roles? If not, what's missing? What gaps in knowledge, talent, and expertise do you need to fill?

Suppose, for example, 70% of a marketing firm's revenue comes from RFP (request for proposal) bids. The challenge with winning RFP business is that it usually means you're the lowest bidder.

But if the goal is to grow revenue from $10 million to $50 million in the next five years, something has to change. Continuing the low-bid sales process won't work. It's too unpredictable and unprofitable to achieve exponential growth.

The company must shift from dependence on RFPs to a business development model. This approach expands growth potential by building long-term prospect and client relationships. It's more intentional, strategic, and conducive to predicting sales. And it's less reliant on the low conversion percentage of competitive bids.

So, what roles should you fill to shift the company's sales from 70% bids to 70% business development? At this point, you would focus on building a more robust sales team to achieve the goal.

2. Do we have the right people in their optimal roles?

As you review each position, is the best person in that role? If not, why? Do you need to change your lineup? Who should you shift around? Who should you replace?

You might discover some employees who thrived in a previous role but now seem out of place. For example, think of the rock star salesperson whose success got them promoted to VP of Sales. But they lack the leadership skills to build a high-performance sales team.

Or, you could uncover gems. You might discover your receptionist has the skills to flourish in a marketing role.

But how do you get people to open up about their desired role? Try this question: *If given the opportunity that you currently do not have to impact the business, what would that impact be?*

A 360-degree review can also help uncover an employee's optimal role. These reviews get feedback from supervisors, peers, and direct reports. And they compare that feedback with the employee's self-assessment. The result is a clearer picture of each team member's capabilities and interests. This way, you can slot them in the best role—for both them and the company.

3. How should we incentivize key people to ensure those roles stay filled?

The competition is fierce for top talent. What executive compensation and benefits tools can help you keep your best employees? How can you better align executive incentives with company performance?

You might think, "But where do we find the money to pay for these retention programs?" But consider the flip side of that question: "What's the cost if we *don't* keep our most valuable players?"

The idea here is that smart investments in talent retention will more than pay for themselves.

Humility & Role Optimization

What, exactly, does Humility have to do with Role Optimization?

The exercise requires self-awareness, open-mindedness, and confidence. Usually, the discovery of our optimal roles comes from a 360-feedback process. And it takes Humility to receive feedback with an open mind.

In other words, all participants must practice Humility. That's why Role Optimization is not easy. Everyone needs to be on the same page and open to change. But when you commit to making that happen through the practice of Humility, the payoff will be enormous.

The Bottom Line

If you want to build a high-performing company, lead with Humility. Be the gardener, not the chess master. Break the grip of Egotism through self-awareness. Move out of the "center of the circle" to empower your team to take the initiative and free you to do what you do best. And then get the right people in the right roles, rowing in the right direction.

When you lead with Humility, you create the "fertile soil" in which the Collaboration Effect on Profit can flourish.

In the Trenches: Blinded by Egotism

David Harper

Egotism is easy to point out in others but hard to see in ourselves. If we're unaware, Egotism *will* take its toll on even our most cherished relationships.

I've seen it happen time and time again in my own life. I'm sure you've seen it affect your relationships, as well.

An example that hits home for me is this. I took our adult sons on a ski trip to Colorado a few years ago. At the time, we were having some undercurrents of misunderstanding within our family. I figured the issue was among our kids. So, I planned on being the one to "facilitate" this discussion among the men, and we'll just hash it out!

Little did I know a large chunk of the "misunderstanding" had to do with me. Of course, I didn't see it! That's what Egotism does!

So, as we headed toward the slopes in the car, I was in for a surprise. One of my sons said, "Dad, we think you and Mom need to go to counseling. We've all been to counseling, and it's been helpful to us."

What? The only people in our generation who went to counseling were people who had serious marriage issues, which my wife, Anne, and I did not have!

I immediately resisted the idea in my mind. *"Why do I need to go to counseling? I'm not the one causing these issues!"*

Or, so I thought. The reality is I couldn't see it because of Egotism.

I don't remember exactly how the switch happened in my head. But I could feel myself soften. My initial irritation and defensiveness began to wane. You could say the virtue of Humility was at work, starting to open my heart and my eyes to the situation.

To make a long story short, Anne and I did go to counseling, and we're both glad we did! We discovered significant things about ourselves that helped strengthen our marriage—and our relationships with our children.

I learned that, with my strong personality, I tend to want to control everything—and everybody! I tend to be impatient, unkind, and not gentle. To be the best version of myself, I needed to demonstrate the opposite of my tendencies—what the Bible calls "the fruits of the Spirit," like patience, kindness, and gentleness.

It was time for me to "let go" and stop trying to control things with our children. After all, they were successful adults in their own right. I didn't need to give them unsolicited advice. Instead, they needed me to be patient and let them come to me when they needed my counsel.

As you can imagine, much of this was hard to hear. But, wow! It was what I needed. It was what my family needed.

We've since been able to talk things through and begin experiencing healing in our family. But none of this would have happened if Egotism had its way.

Deeper Reflection

1. How do you think Egotism has shaped your leadership style up to this point?

2. In what ways has Egotism undermined your ability to get the most out of your team?

3. What is the cost to your company if you allow Egotism to fester in yourself and your team?

4. How can you become a more effective gardener (vs. chess master)? What would that look like in your company?

5. On a scale of 1 to 10, with 10 being the highest, how would you rate your level of Humility? What would you need to change to move your rating from your current number to a 10?

6. If you were serving in the role that best fits your skills and interests, what would that role be?

7. Is that your role today? If not, what would your ideal role look like? What adjustments should you make to allow you to work in your optimal role?

8. What about your team? Do you have all the roles you need to fill to achieve your mission?

9. Are all your people serving in their optimal roles? If not, what changes should you make to your lineup?

10. What is your incentive strategy for employee retention? How is it working? What steps can you take to shore up your incentive programs?

Remember:

Ego is the enemy. Practice Humility to open your mind to consider new ways of doing things. That's when you'll discover the breakthrough ideas you've been searching for.

CHAPTER 4:
VIRTUE #2: EMPATHY VS. BUSYNESS

> *"When we focus on ourselves, our world contracts as our problems and preoccupations loom large. But when we focus on others, our world expands. Our own problems drift to the periphery of the mind and so seem smaller, and we increase our capacity for connection."*
> *- Daniel Goldman, Social Intelligence:*
> *The New Science of Human Relationships*

Remember the Bible story about the Good Samaritan? A mugger beat, robbed, and left a man to die on the roadside. A priest approached the victim but looked away and walked right past him. Another religious leader did the same thing. He kept walking.

Then came a Samaritan. People in the victim's community viewed Samaritans with contempt as unwelcome foreigners. But the "enemy" Samaritan stopped to help anyway. He tended to the man's wounds, carried him to a safe place for medical attention, and paid for his care.

Most discussion about this story focuses on the Good Samaritan's compassion. And rightfully so. But in this chapter, we'll also shine the spotlight on the two religious leaders who kept walking.

After all, a big part of their job was to help those in need. So, why did they walk past the man clinging to life?

The Bible doesn't give the details. But we can infer a reason why they didn't stop: **They were "too busy" to care.**

Trapped by Good Intentions

Now, it's easy to wag a finger at the priests for being pompous hypocrites.

But be careful. As a business owner, you're especially vulnerable to falling into the trap of being too busy:

- Too busy to notice when employees are burning out.
- Too busy to see the widening rift between you and your spouse.
- Too busy to sense that your kids and grandkids are starving for your attention.

While we don't know what the priests were thinking in the Good Samaritan story, we can imagine they, too, had good intentions.

- *"The worship service is in two hours. I need to prep my sermon and don't have time to stop."*

- *"This fundraiser is make-or-break for us, and I'm the main reason the donors are coming. I can't risk missing it and letting our team down."*

- *"I'm leading a city-wide prayer meeting in 30 minutes. I must get there on time. I can't stop."*

You're thinking, "Those are lame excuses!" Yes, they are. But aren't we all prone to giving similar excuses—just in a different context that's more "acceptable" to us? Think about it:

Do you ever break promises with your spouse and kids because of work?

- The excuse: *"But I'm doing whatever it takes to provide for my family. They'll understand."*

Do you ever put off meetings with a struggling employee while you're dealing with one crisis after another?

- The excuse: *"But I have to put out these fires first!"*

Do you ever push employees past their breaking point because you're too busy to see it coming?

- The excuse: *"Look! I can't read minds. If people have issues with something, they should come to me. In the meantime, I've got payroll to make!"*

Like the priests, you feel like you're doing the right thing. But, in reality, you're in the grip of the vice of Busyness, which will squeeze the life out of you and your company if you don't break free.

Busyness Defined

What is Busyness?

It's not the same thing as "being busy." After all, there's virtue in hard work. But when your work consumes you, *that's* when "busy" crosses the line to Busyness.

As Stephen Covey puts it: "How many people on their deathbed wish they spent more time in the office?" That question puts life and business in proper perspective.

But it's easy to lose that mindset when you're at the office and have this nagging feeling to stay and keep working. "It's not like I'll be going at this pace forever," you rationalize. "I'll put in the long hours now to free me up later."

But "later" never arrives. Something else keeps coming up, requiring more and more of your time and attention.

That's Busyness. If left unchecked, it will consume you–and the people around you.

Busyness at Scale: High-Drama, Low-Trust Culture

What happens when Busyness spreads beyond the owner to infect the entire team?

Consider this quote by Dr. Richard Swenson in *Margin: Restoring Emotional, Physical, Financial, and Time Reserves to Overloaded Lives*: "Our relationships are being starved to death by velocity. No one has the time to listen, let alone love."

Busyness is "velocity" that starves your relationships with key leaders.

Think about it. Whenever you feel overwhelmed, don't you get tunnel vision—where all you see are the urgent problems immediately before you? If so, that's a normal—and often healthy—response to certain high-stress situations. It's a way that we can block out distractions and focus on the tasks at hand to solve the problem.

But when you operate in a chronic state of Busyness, that coping mechanism causes more harm than good. Your "velocity," as Swenson puts it, starves key relationships and kills productivity. That's because when your team needs your input, you're "too busy" to give their requests much thought.

"Just handle it!" you tell them. But they don't know where to start. And as their workload piles up, the Busyness cycle accelerates. It spreads throughout the team. Now everyone feels overwhelmed and on edge.

If this cycle persists, it produces a toxic culture marked by high drama and low trust. Employees walk on eggshells, trying to figure out where they fit within the organization.

Fighting Off Busyness with Empathy

So, how can you break this vicious cycle of Busyness? How can you become more like the Good Samaritan and less like the priests?

Practice Empathy, the second of the Great 8 Virtues. Empathy forces you to slow down your mind. It helps you see what is most important, not only for yourself but also for your people. You begin to understand the big picture. You notice how your performance impacts the ability of others on the team to do their jobs. You recognize when your team feels overwhelmed. And you make time to help them navigate their challenges and achieve their goals.

Empathy = Strength

Before we go further, let's address some misconceptions about Empathy. It does *not* mean:

- Getting caught up in someone else's drama
- Letting someone off the hook
- Going against your values
- Getting sucked into a guilt trip
- Agreeing with their opinions
- Accepting their behavior.

These are examples of weakness, insecurity, and gullibility. Those traits have nothing to do with Empathy.

Instead, Empathy is strength. It's the strength to respect people—no matter what—without bringing yourself down. It's the strength to listen without judgment so you can see the world through their eyes. At times, it's also the strength to push past your feelings to help someone who may have hurt you.

And that's precisely the strength the Good Samaritan showed—the strength to put his schedule on hold to try to save the life of someone who likely considered him an enemy.

Putting Empathy into Practice

How can you break the back of Busyness with the strength of Empathy?

Here are five steps—the "Five Rs"—for putting Empathy into daily practice:

1. Recognize.

We all get busy from time to time. That's normal. The problem arises when we're "too busy" to be present when interacting with others. So, create an early detection system. This way, when your schedule starts to get out of hand, you can do something about it.

2. Resist.

Refuse to treat Busyness as a badge of honor. Instead, see it for what it is. It's a vice that keeps you from executing your highest priorities.

3. Reconnect.

When you feel things are getting out of kilter, take a step back to reconnect with your vision. Do those activities align with your personal and organizational "Why"? If not, what do you need to do right now to reconnect with that purpose?

4. Recalibrate.

Take a step back from all the pressures vying for your attention to refocus and recalibrate your priorities. This frees you to give your full attention to the right people and tasks.

5. Reach out.

Look for opportunities to reach out to your team and take a genuine interest in their work and lives. Discover what they get excited about and what concerns them the most. When you understand your team's perspective, you learn how to help them succeed.

Empathy at Scale: Most Important Tasks (MITs)

How do you instill Empathy throughout your company?

That's where MITs—Most Important Tasks—come into play.

MITs empower you and your team to create margin—that is, free up time—to operate with more Empathy and less Busyness. The idea is to identify the two to three most important tasks you must complete each week that make the most significant impact on your company's success.

You may be thinking, "But I've got 50 things I *must* do this week!" If that's the case, you need to delegate or cut most of those items. Otherwise, you'll be stuck in the vicious cycle of Busyness. Instead, identify your highest leverage and highest impact tasks. "Let's get these three things right. These are the most important for our business."

What do MITs look like?

Take, for example, a chief operating officer for one of our clients at Legacy. He had several division vice presidents reporting to him. But when they needed his input, he was "too busy" to respond within a reasonable timeframe.

So, one of his MITs looked like this: "Assess every deliverable or request my VPs need from me and respond by the end of the day each Friday."

If you're a project manager at a construction company, one MIT might be: "Review all invoices by seven days before the invoice due date."

Or, if you're a sales rep, an MIT might be: "Make 20 'touches' with new prospects by the end of the day Thursday of each week."

Developing MITs

Each MIT example above follows the "SMART Goal" format. They're:

- **Specific:** *Does the MIT represent a defined deliverable?*

- **Measurable:** *Is it something we can measure so we can track progress?*

- **Attainable:** *Is it realistic?*

- **Relevant:** *Does it align with the company's broader strategy?*

- **Time-Bound:** *What is the deadline?*

Go back to the COO example. "Assess every deliverable or request that my VPs need from me and respond by the end of the day each Friday."

Let's break down this MIT using the SMART model:

- **Specific?** Yes. "Assess every deliverable my VPs need from me."

- **Measurable?** Yes. "Respond to every request." This doesn't always mean that he completes the deliverable. But it does mean that he responds to each request.

- **Attainable?** Yes. This MIT is realistic and doable.

- **Relevant?** Yes. This is critical to the job and success of the company—to support the VPs who are leading teams on the ground. Moreover, the COO needs to know the pulse of what's going on with the divisions to articulate that "pulse" to the CEO.

- **Time-Bound?** Yes. The deadline is "by the end of the day each Friday."

Now, there may be occasions where you won't be able to develop a complete response by the Friday deadline. And that's okay, as long you communicate that to your VP. You might say, "I want to keep you in the loop. This task is on my list, but I can't get to it by 3:00 pm today. I should be able to get back to you by Monday."

Aligning Individual and Team MITs

Once you've chosen your MITs, it's time to take the MIT development process to the next step: The group session.

This is where each person shares their MITs with the others on the team to get their input and feedback.

After all, it's one thing to set your priorities. But as you share your MITs and listen to the others share theirs, you begin to understand the big picture. You see how interdependent each person's role is to the entire organization's success.

For example, imagine you're the CFO of a construction company. You've determined that one of your MITs each week is to pay all invoices for your subcontractors due that week. If your subcontractors don't get paid on time, that's not good for business and your company's reputation.

But who's responsible for giving you those invoices? That depends on the organization. But let's say, in this case, it's the project manager. Your MITs rely on the project manager to review the invoices and send them to you. This means the project manager needs to set an MIT like this: "Review all invoices by seven days before the invoice due date."

But that's only one half of the equation. Who's responsible for invoicing clients? After all, you need the cash flow to pay the subcontractors on time. Again, in this case, that's likely to be the project manager's responsibility, as well.

You can see where this is going. Suppose the CFO and project manager are not on the same page about each other's MITs. That misalignment would cause a breakdown in their capacity to do their jobs.

Following Through on MITs

But developing MITs cannot be a "set-it-and-forget-it" exercise. It requires consistent check-ins to ensure everyone follows through on their commitments. And that includes you, the owner.

As retired Navy SEAL Jocko Willink writes in *Extreme Ownership: How U.S. Navy SEALS Lead and Win*, "You don't get what you preach, you get what you tolerate."

Our leadership team at Legacy helps each other stay on track by taking a few minutes to discuss our MITs during our weekly meeting. We go around the table. If you fulfilled all your MITs, you give a thumbs up. And if you didn't get to all your tasks, you give a thumbs down.

This portion of our meeting creates an environment where you take ownership of your performance. After all, you don't want to arrive at the meeting having to give a thumbs down if you can do anything about it. And excuses will only compound the problem. So, the weekly meeting reminds you to stay focused on completing your MITs during the week.

But if you encounter problems, these weekly meetings can also help you get back on track. Things happen that may require you to make "in-game" adjustments. And that's the value of regular checkups. They allow for feedback and discussion to change course as necessary.

MITs help you and your team understand each person's roles and goals. And that's the essence of Empathy. You're able to look beyond yourself to see the world through other people's eyes. That high level of understanding is the key to building trust among your team—and building momentum for the Collaboration Effect on Profit.

The Bottom Line

How can you tell if a company practices Empathy?

You'll see it in people's faces when you walk in the door. You'll see employees smiling, laughing, and enjoying themselves and their work. They're not frowning or giving off a vibe that management treats them like an object. They're excited about being a part of a team that recognizes their contributions to the company's success.

But Empathy doesn't just happen. It requires intentionality to break free from Busyness. That's why MITs are so important. They help you create margin, giving you more time to develop high-trust relationships. And the more people can trust you, the more you can connect with them, influence them, and help them achieve great things.

In the Trenches: 'Mind Over Matter'

David Harper

I used to be late for meetings—all of the time!

I thought if I could cram just a few more things into my schedule, I'd be more effective and successful. At least, that's how I justified my lateness.

I embraced Busyness as a badge of honor. But I was hurting my relationships with my team, clients, and partners because I communicated that I didn't respect them or their time.

Then one day in the mid-1980s, I attended a management training conference where I heard a phrase that changed my perspective—and behavior. The speaker said something along these lines:

*"You've heard of the phrase, 'Life is about mind over matter,' right? Well...when someone is late, what they're really communicating is this: 'I don't **mind** (being late) and you (having to wait) don't **matter!**"*

Those words hit me hard. I was so caught up with myself and my own "to-do's" that I didn't consider how I was treating those I kept waiting—like they didn't matter.

I thought, "How can I keep doing this to people *all the time?*" And the more I reflected, the more I realized that even after I finally arrived at the meetings, I struggled to be truly present with those people. And they could feel it.

That's what the vice of Busyness does. It squeezes your schedule, starves your relationships, and stifles your productivity.

I learned that Busyness is *not* a badge of honor. It's a trap that we must break free of before it's too late!

That's where the virtue of Empathy comes in. It breaks the grip of Busyness over your life. When you start practicing Empathy, you don't ever want to be late again because you're in tune with how that makes other people feel. So you do everything you can to seize control over your schedule and manage it realistically.

That's why we stress the importance of developing your Most Important Tasks (MITs), which we break down for you in this chapter. Your MITs allow you to create the margin in your schedule for Empathy to flourish—and transform the dynamic between you and your team.

When you show Empathy, people feel it. They can sense when you're fully present with them, intently listening, and genuinely caring about what they have to say.

In that moment, you're telling them that **they matter.**

Deeper Reflection

1. Reflect on the Good Samaritan story. What areas in your life and business do you think make you the most vulnerable to being more like the priest and less like the Samaritan?

COLLABORATION EFFECT ON PROFIT

2. Why? What is it about those areas that make you especially prone to Busyness?

3. To what extent has Busyness affected your leadership effectiveness?

4. What's at stake? What's the cost to you and your company if you don't break free from the Busyness trap?

5. Who is a successful person you point to as an excellent role model for practicing Empathy? How do they do it?

6. On a scale of 1 to 10, with 10 being the highest, how would you rate your level of Empathy? What would you need to change to move your rating from your current number to a 10?

7. What are your MITs—and are they SMART?

8. Does your team know *their* MITs?

9. What's your process for holding each other accountable for completing MITs?

10. Imagine you and your team have broken free from Busyness and are practicing Empathy at a high level. What would that look like? How would you describe the difference in your company? What would be the impact on your bottom line?

> **Remember:**
>
> *Busyness is toxic to your company's long-term success. So, practice Empathy to create the margin you need to develop your people into a powerhouse team.*

74

CHAPTER 5:
VIRTUE #3: ATTENTIVENESS VS. DISTRACTION

"The successful warrior is the average man, with laser-like focus."

- Bruce Lee

It was 7:18 pm on January 13, 2012. The Costa Concordia departed the Port of Rome for a seven-day cruise on the Mediterranean Sea.

Smooth waters. Calm skies. Breathtaking views. All was well for the 4,200 passengers and crew on board. But in two and a half hours, their lives—and the ship—would be upended.

Capt. Francesco Schettino directed the Concordia on a slight detour for a "sail-by" off the coast of Giglio Island. A sail-by is a risky maneuver where a cruise ship sails close to land to give passengers a good view.

As the ship approached the island, the married captain invited his mistress to the command center to show her the beautiful coastline. At 9:45 pm, he was on a phone call to a friend onshore when *BAM!* The ship came to a violent halt.

It struck a reef that tore a 50-meter gash into the hull. Water burst into the engine room and shorted out the electrical system. The ship went dark.

Capt. Schettino panicked. At first, he downplayed the damage to the Italian Coast Guard. He told them the ship only experienced a blackout and was not taking on water. But reports show he knew otherwise. This decision delayed rescue efforts by 30 minutes.

Chaos ensued. As the ship took on more and more water, it began listing (tilting) toward the starboard (right) side. But Capt. Schettino didn't issue the evacuation order until over an hour after impact.

A few hours later, the once majestic Concordia took its last gasp. It tilted onto its side and rested in the shallow waters off the island's coast.

Thirty-two people perished.

What happened? What caused the Concordia disaster?

It wasn't rough seas. It wasn't bad weather. It wasn't faulty equipment.

According to officials, it was human error. Capt. Schettino got distracted, which impaired his judgment. And his decisions set off a cascade of catastrophic events that didn't have to happen.

All It Takes is Once

What can founders learn from the Concordia disaster?

The story offers many leadership lessons—of what *not* to do. But the biggest takeaway is an uncomfortable truth: *We are all more like Capt. Schettino than we would ever want to admit.*

We all get distracted. And he got distracted by things that could trip any of us. Consider the first officer's court testimony about the chaos before the collision:

> *[Capt. Schettino] arrived in the command center accompanied by a woman, then gave an order to switch to manual control of the helm. But he did not immediately speak the phrase 'I'm taking control,' which signals a change in command. However, given the way he positioned himself, I assumed he had taken command and I thought I was no longer in charge. Then, since the captain was distracted, and we were getting close to Giglio, I gave orders to the helmsman.*

Beware of Becoming *That* Boss

Sound familiar?

A version of this scenario happens all the time in companies. There's confusion. The boss is distracted. The employee tries to get the boss' attention to clarify instructions but is ignored. As the situation escalates, the employee feels the need to step in and make a call. And that's when bad things happen—when the boss gets distracted.

Have you ever worked with a distracted boss like that? Have you ever *been* that boss?

"Okay. Sure. But if I were Capt. Schettino, I would never get distracted like that with thousands of people's lives in my hands!" you protest.

Perhaps. But we're all human.

Think about it. Before 9:45 pm on January 13, 2012, Capt. Schettino likely thought he had everything under control. Why not? He was a veteran ship captain with a clean service record.

But when it comes to the vice of Distraction, all it takes is one time. One moment. One lapse in judgment. And BAM! Everything changes.

You're the captain of your company. Your employees have their financial future in your hands. If you get distracted and run your company into the ground, your people will get hurt.

Distraction Defined

What is Distraction?

It's taking your eye off the proverbial ball—your mission, your team, and your priorities. That's when you become most prone to making costly mistakes.

Capt. Schettino took his eye off his mission by initiating the sail-by to impress his new girlfriend. He took his eye off his team during the sail-by when he failed to confirm who was responsible for piloting the vessel to avoid the rocks. Then, he took his eye off his priorities after the collision. He focused more on covering up his mistakes than on saving lives.

Imagine if Capt. Schettino had kept his eye on the ball that fateful night. What if he had chosen to stay on course, not do the sail-by? No dangerous rocks. No collision. No lives lost. He might still be captain today with many commendations.

As the captain of your company, you make critical decisions every day. And so many things are vying for attention. Perhaps it's drama in your personal life. Or it's a toxic employee. Or it's the fear of losing a key leader or a big customer. Or, it's all the above, all at once.

Whatever it is, stay alert. Keep your eye on the ball. Confront and deal with issues. Otherwise, the vice of Distraction could sink your business when you least expect it.

Distraction at Scale: Rowing in Different Directions

What happens when Distraction spreads beyond the owner to infect the entire team?

Consider the story of *Alice in Wonderland*. In one scene, Alice arrives at a fork in the road, where she sees a Cheshire cat sitting in the tree.

"Which road do I take?" she asks.

"Where do you want to go?" the cat responds.

"I don't know."

"Then it doesn't matter," the cat says.

The lesson? If you don't have a clear direction in mind, your company will become vulnerable to Distraction:

- *Should we change strategy or stay the course?*
- *Should we shift resources to this product or that?*

How do you answer these questions if you and your team aren't on the same page about where to take the business?

After all, whatever you decide, as the Cheshire cat said, "It doesn't matter."

As a result, the company gets sucked into a vortex of Distraction. Leadership lurches from one new "flavor-of-the-month" strategy to another, hoping something will stick. Employees get sidetracked because they keep having to change course.

Over time, a culture of chronic Distraction takes a heavy toll on the business. It becomes harder to get everyone rowing in the same direction. And that chaos undermines your ability to compete against more focused, disciplined companies.

Fighting off Distraction with Attentiveness

How can you fight Distraction? How can you keep your eye on the ball and avoid a Capt. Schettino moment?

Practice Attentiveness, the third of the Great 8 Virtues. Attentiveness:

- Focuses your attention on the goal

- Makes you more decisive

- Reduces "boneheaded" mistakes

- Keeps you calm under pressure.

When defining Attentiveness, consider this word: **"Praus" [prah-oos]**. It's a military term from ancient Greece that describes a mighty warhorse. This horse is special because it can anticipate its rider's movements in even the most chaotic situations.

In contrast, untrained horses get skittish in battle and resist the rider. This misalignment between horse and rider puts the mission—and their lives—at risk.

A Praus warhorse stays calm in the chaos. It focuses on one thing: To move as "one" with its rider. And that's what the virtue of Attentiveness looks like in action. You're the warhorse. The "rider" is your vision. Your job is to align your efforts—and your team's—to follow where that bold vision leads.

(To dig deeper, check out *Praus: A Parable for Winning the War Within* by our long-time friend Hunter Lambeth.)

Attentiveness = Concentrated Energy

Before we go further, let's address some misconceptions about Attentiveness. It does *not* mean:

- Being unwilling to change course despite the facts
- Making a blind commitment to a losing strategy
- Closing your mind to new ideas that threaten the status quo
- Suppressing dissenting opinions to force consensus.

These are examples of being defensive—afraid of losing control. Attentiveness is *not* staying committed to a bad strategy. That's stubbornness.

Instead, Attentiveness is about going on offense. It's about concentrating energy on achieving a bold and worthy vision.

Think of Attentiveness as a magnifying glass. It concentrates the sun's energy into a single point so hot that it burns a hole into paper. When we allow Distraction to take hold, we diffuse our energy and make little impact. But when we focus our efforts on a specific target, we generate the force we need to achieve big goals.

Putting Attentiveness into Practice

How can you protect your blindside from Distraction with Attentiveness?

Here are five steps for putting Attentiveness into daily practice:

1. Perform a Distraction audit.

What aspects in your life are—or could be—taking your eye off the proverbial ball? Personal drama? Toxic relationships? Substance abuse? Family problems? Financial troubles? Social media addiction? Fear? Doubt? All the above? Be candid with yourself. You can't take out a target unless you can see it.

2. Counteract each issue.

Develop a plan for dealing with each issue that makes you vulnerable to Distraction. Work on that plan each day. Adjust it until you're satisfied that you can keep the problem in check.

3. Plan for interruptions.

Be intentional about how you handle interruptions from your team. If it's a genuine emergency, that's one thing. But for most other requests that can wait a bit, block out time each day when you're free to deal with those items. Think of it like "office hours." Your team knows you're available in specific time blocks to respond to requests and take "Do you have a minute?" conversations.

4. Clarify your vision and mission.

When you're unclear on your priorities, you must figure out what to do next. This hesitation makes you vulnerable to getting distracted by other people's agendas.

5. Create alignment.

Does your schedule align with your vision? If not, what tasks or appointments should you delegate or eliminate to get on track? The idea is to connect the dots between your daily to-do list and your goals.

Attentiveness at Scale: Line of Sight

How do you instill Attentiveness throughout your company?

Give your team Line of Sight to the company's targets.

As the owner, you have a clear Line of Sight, but others on the team often get left in the dark. As a result, even the most talented employees won't perform at the level you'd expect.

Why?

It goes back to the Cheshire cat's insight: If you don't know where you're going, any road will do.

If team members don't see what they're working towards, how do they know whether they're making progress? They don't have a clear vision to help guide their decisions–what they should say Yes or No to. So, they get distracted by unproductive tasks, turf wars, and office politics. They take their eye off the ball because they don't know what that "ball" is.

With Line of Sight, employees can focus on helping the company hit its targets. As John Doerr writes in *Measure What*

Matters, "Contributors are most engaged when they can see how their work contributes to the company's success. Quarter to quarter, day to day, they look for tangible measures of their achievement."

How do you create an environment that promotes Line of Sight? Establish a productive meeting routine for reviewing progress toward the company's targets.

Patrick Lencioni recommends four types of meetings in *Death by Meeting: A Leadership Fable...About Solving the Most Painful Problem in Business*. Each meeting type has a unique goal, duration, and agenda.

1. Daily Check-Ins

Think of this meeting as a daily "huddle." Everyone is standing; you don't want anyone sitting down and getting comfortable. Keep the meeting to five minutes, where you share daily schedules and activities. And don't cancel even when some people can't be there.

"[The Daily Check-In] provides a quick forum for ensuring that nothing falls through the cracks on a given day and that no one steps on anyone else's toes," Lencioni says. "Just as important, it helps eliminate the need for unnecessary and time-consuming email chains about schedule coordination."

But remember that the Daily Check-In won't work for every organization. As Lencioni puts it, "Teams should commit to doing Daily Check-Ins for a set period—perhaps two months—before evaluating whether or not they are working."

2. Weekly Tactical

These meetings run 45 to 90 minutes to discuss weekly activities, metrics, and tactical issues. But don't set the agenda until after team members have each given their 60-second report and progress review.

Lencioni recommends this structure for a successful Weekly Tactical meeting:

- **Lightning Round:** Each key team member gives a 60-second report of their work that week. "What are the three things you're doing this week?"

- **Progress Review:** "How did you do last week?"

- **Real-Time Agenda:** Use the Lightning Round and Progress Review discussion to set the agenda in real-time. Limit the conversation to topics that immediately impact tactical issues and goals. If a new strategic topic does not fit the Weekly Tactical framework, move it to the Monthly Strategic meeting.

3. Monthly Strategic

These meetings run for about two to four hours. Unlike the Weekly Tactical, you should prepare an agenda limited to one, two, or, at most, three topics. The purpose: discuss, debate, brainstorm, and decide upon critical issues affecting long-term success.

4. Quarterly Off-Site Review

Take one or two days to step back from the daily, weekly, and monthly grind to review things from a distance. Possible topics:

- Changes in the competitive landscape

- Employee morale

- Executive team dynamics

- Top and bottom performers

- Customer satisfaction

- Everything that has a long-term impact on the company.

"Executives should regularly assess themselves and their behaviors as a team, identifying trends or tendencies that may not be serving the organization," Lencioni writes. "This often requires a change in scenery so that executives can interact with one another on a more personal level and remind themselves of their collective commitments to the team."

The Bottom Line

What does it look like when you practice the virtue of Attentiveness?

You're doing the right things in an excellent way. You're concentrating your energy on the few tasks that make the most significant impact. And you're protecting yourself—and the company—from a Capt. Schettino moment.

The result?

Increased productivity. Better decision-making. A happier and more fulfilled team working together, all rowing in the same direction.

It's a picture of the Collaboration Effect on Profit in motion.

In the Trenches: Distracted By Focus

David Harper

Nick (not his real name) was a shareholder and the top producer in the consulting firm. But there was a problem: Nick was also difficult to work with.

"We don't know what to do with him. He's not a good partner," the company's other shareholders said.

Nick was preoccupied and aloof in meetings, not engaged in conversations that really needed his attention. Despite working a ton of hours, he became a bottleneck to the company's growth. He was unwilling to "let go" and delegate, believing he was the only one who could get the work done right.

His wife pleaded with him, "Why are you driving yourself so hard? I wish we could go on a trip– just the two of us and just be together. But here it is, a Friday night at 9:00, and you're still at the office!"

That's what Founder's Syndrome looks like. You see yourself as the only one who can do the job. And do it, you will…until your team, family, and health become collateral damage.

During our first coaching session, Nick told me, "I'm wired to be the best in everything." And that explains why it was so hard for him to let certain things go and be a team player.

On the surface, he appeared absolutely focused. But his problem was the exact opposite: He was distracted.

What was the source of Nick's battle with Distraction?

It's the same for many of us Type-A personalities—Ambition. That is, when it crosses the line to selfish ambition. As Philippians 2:3-4 says, "Do nothing out of selfish ambition or empty conceit, but with humility of mind consider others as more important than yourself. Do not merely look out for your own interests but also the interests of others."

Nick was distracted by an obsession to fulfill his own interests without considering the impact of his actions on other people—and their interests.

During our coaching sessions, we'd talk about how he could apply The Great 8 Virtues to his life—starting with the virtue of Attentiveness.

Since then, Nick began a transformation process where he has:

- Become a good partner and effective leader in the firm

- Reduced his hours to a more sustainable 40-50 hours per week

- Learned to "let go," delegating a whole lot more than he ever imagined to his team

- Started taking some long weekends to go on trips with his wife.

Nick said, "Now that I've tasted living like this [with The Great 8 Virtues], I'm never going back!"

Deeper Reflection

1. Reflect on the lesson of the Costa Concordia story. What distractions in your life *right now* make you vulnerable to a Capt. Schettino moment?

2. Why? What is it about those areas that make you especially prone to Distraction?

3. To what extent has Distraction affected your leadership effectiveness?

4. What's at stake? What's the cost to you and your company if you don't keep the vice of Distraction in check?

5. Who can you point to as an excellent role model for practicing Attentiveness? What are the signs of Attentiveness you see in them?

6. On a scale of 1 to 10, with 10 being the highest, how would you rate your Attentiveness? What would you need to change to move your rating from your current number to a 10?

7. Does your team have Line of Sight to company targets?

8. Do they understand how their role impacts the company's success?

9. Does your company's meeting cadence promote a clear Line of Sight, or does it get in the way?

10. Imagine you and your team are practicing Attentiveness

at a high level. What would that look like? How would you describe the difference in your company? What would be the impact on your bottom line?

Remember:

When it comes to Distraction, all it takes is one moment to upend your company, your life, and the lives of those around you. So, practice Attentiveness to keep your business and life on course.

CHAPTER 6:
VIRTUE #4: ACCOUNTABILITY VS. GREED

"Responsibility equals accountability equals ownership. And a sense of ownership is the most powerful weapon a team or organization can have."
- Coach Pat Summitt

t's an iconic scene in Oliver Stone's 1987 movie *Wall Street*. Michael Douglas plays the corporate raider Gordon Gekko.

His target: Teldar Paper. The scene: Teldar's shareholder's meeting.

It's a packed house. The company's chief executive finished presenting his case for rejecting Gekko's hostile takeover. Now it's Gekko's turn to speak. As he grabs the mic, his presence fills the room. And so do his words as he closes his speech by delivering one of the most memorable lines in movie history:

The point is, ladies and gentlemen, that greed–for lack of a better word–is good.

Greed is right.

Greed works.

Greed clarifies, cuts through, and captures the essence of the evolutionary spirit.

Greed, in all of its forms–greed for life, for money, for love, knowledge–has marked the upward surge of mankind.

And greed–you mark my words–will not only save Teldar Paper, but that other malfunctioning corporation called the USA.

Those words won over the crowd as he basked in their rousing applause. But that scene would also mark Gekko's high point in the movie.

He soon learns that enriching himself at the expense of others would cause his life to unravel.

Instead of marking the "upward surge of mankind," the vice of Greed shoves Gekko to his downfall. And he would spend the next several years in prison for insider trading and securities fraud.

The moral: Greed is *not* good, no matter how you spin it. It's bad. It destroys lives, depletes wealth, and derails businesses. And it's a vice that could threaten your company's future without you seeing it coming.

The Subtlety of Greed

Gordon Gekko is an extreme example of Greed. So, it's easy to point the finger and say, "I would never be like him!" But consider these more subtle examples that can be easier to justify:

- Tolerating a manager's toxic behavior because they're "too valuable"

- Taking on more clients than the company can serve properly

- Blocking employees from sharing in the wealth they've helped create for the company

- Cutting a sales rep's compensation because they're "making too much money"

- Subjecting employees to abusive clients who are "too profitable to lose."

Do you ever wrestle with scenarios like these? Take a step back and be candid with yourself. Get in tune with the potential influence Greed has on your decision-making. This way, you'll gain greater insight into how to counteract it.

The Elephant in the Room

Another subtle example: What will happen to the business when you retire?

It's the elephant in the room. Your key leaders are thinking about it. So are their direct reports.

What's going to happen to the business in the long term? Who will take over the helm? Are they selling the company?

If you're like most business owners, you're not ready to talk about it. You think, "What happens if I share my thoughts? Won't my best people leave? That will crush the business!"

See where Greed begins to get a foothold? On one level, it seems justified. You believe that by keeping your cards close to the vest, you're doing what's best for the company—to ensure your top people don't leave.

But if you're brutally honest, you'll see Greed's influence on your thinking: "I can't afford to lose anyone right now. This would drop the value of the asset I've worked so hard to build. I can't let that happen."

Sure, you must be wise with what you share, when, and with whom. But you also don't want to mislead your team because you withheld information they deserved to know.

The irony is that Greed will diminish your company's value, not protect it. While you may not want to discuss the future, everyone else is anxious about it. And they'll become distracted, wasting productive time worrying about their future and looking for other jobs.

(We break down a High-Trust Communication approach for broaching this specific topic in Chapter 8:"Virtue #6: Integrity vs. Dishonesty.")

Greed Defined

What is Greed?

Greed is the selfish pursuit of money, sex, and power at the expense of others' interests.

Now, let's be clear. There's nothing wrong with money, sex, and power in themselves. Those are all good things in their proper context. But when you chase them with the wrong motives, that's when they become destructive.

That's because Greed sacrifices principle—and people—on the altar of expedience. It drives zero-sum, win-lose deals. And, if left unchecked, Greed will erode trust with employees, customers, and anyone vital to your company's success.

But what's the difference between Greed and ambition? Don't we need to be ambitious to succeed?

Yes. Unlike Greed, ambition is good. You need ambition to set big goals and achieve great things.

But there's a fine line between ambition and Greed. It's the line between a company becoming a noteworthy success or a cautionary tale.

We cross that line when our ambition becomes self-absorbed. That's when we pursue our goals at the expense of other people. If we're not careful, we'll find ourselves crossing the line and not realizing it until it's too late.

Greed at Scale: Self-Preservation vs. Collaboration

What happens when Greed spreads beyond the owner to infect the entire team?

As Michael Gerber writes in *The E-Myth Revisited: Why Most Small Businesses Don't Work and What to Do About It*, "If you are greedy, your employees will be greedy, giving you less and less of themselves and always asking for more."

A culture of Greed causes employees to shift into self-preservation mode. They no longer feel safe collaborating because they don't trust each other. Nor do they trust the owner. They become more obsessed with "throwing so-and-so under the bus" than building up their teammates.

Maintaining high performance is hard enough with everyone working together. But it's nearly impossible to succeed when leaders and their teams don't trust each other.

Fighting Off Greed with Accountability

How can you break the grip of Greed—and prevent it from ever grabbing hold again?

Practice Accountability, the fourth of the Great 8 Virtues.

Accountability is giving permission to select people to ask the hard questions. It's about opening yourself up to scrutiny: "Look, if you see me acting in ways that don't reflect our values, let me know."

An effective Accountability practice is both vertical and horizontal:

1. Vertical Accountability

The first part of Vertical Accountability is top-down. This is Accountability with your board, advisory board, and outside mentors. It's crucial to select the right people who are strong leaders with high character. Seek their advice, counsel, and feedback consistently. Top-down also includes people under your authority being accountable for fulfilling their agreed-upon action plan.

The second part of Vertical Accountability is bottom-up. This means you're inviting Accountability from those under your authority. This is where you say, "I'm committed to doing everything I say I will do. I will be careful of what I say because, if I say it, I intend to do it. If you see me deviating from the agreed-upon plan and not doing the next right thing in the right way, please bring it to my attention."

This kind of Accountability is rare. And it can only happen if you create an environment where your people feel the psychological safety to speak up without fearing retribution.

One more point on Vertical Accountability: When a leader in authority and their direct report interact on an assignment, and they both agree on the next action, the leader cannot take it back. The handoff has been made, and it cannot be reversed. If the leader takes back the assignment, the whole Accountability system is undermined.

2. Horizontal Accountability

The first part of Horizontal Accountability is with your peers—business leaders you respect who are on a similar level and career path. You meet periodically to hold each other accountable to specific commitments and goals.

The second part is peer Accountability among team members. You're encouraging them to hold each other's feet to the fire. You want them to speak up to one another—when the other party is doing a great job and when they're not.

Accountability Promotes Collaboration

Accountability is also at the heart of The 3 Wins Framework, which we'll unpack later in Part 3 of this book. For now, know that The 3 Wins is a powerful check-and-balance system to block Greed from taking hold.

That's because the essence of The 3 Wins is this: You don't win unless the company and key leaders win, too. You don't pursue your interests at the expense of others. Instead, you do it in alignment and collaboration with others.

That's the spirit that drives the Collaboration Effect on Profit. You and your team will prosper more together than either could do individually under the influence of Greed.

Accountability = Ownership

Before we go further, let's address some misconceptions about Accountability. It does *not* mean:

- Looking to catch people doing wrong
- Shaming people into compliance
- Throwing people under the bus
- Increasing restrictions
- Tracking every minute
- Micromanaging.

These actions erode trust and stifle the Collaboration Effect on Profit. Instead, Accountability is an interactive and timely feedback loop. It offers a safe place to deal with blind spots, build upon strengths, and work through struggles. And it unlocks the highest possible performance in your company. As Corporate trainer Joseph Grenny writes in *Harvard Business Review* (See https://hbr.org/2014/05/the-best-teams-hold-themselves-accountable):

> *"We've found that teams break down in performance roughly as follows:*
>
> - *In the weakest teams, there is no accountability*
> - *In mediocre teams, bosses are the source of accountability*
> - *In high-performance teams, peers manage the vast majority of performance problems with one another."*

Accountability is about taking ownership. You own your performance. Your team owns their results. Together, you help each other raise the entire company's performance. With Accountability, everyone in the company has skin in the game.

Putting Accountability into Practice

How can you break the grip of Greed with Accountability?

Here are three steps for putting Accountability into daily practice:

1. Be open.

This step points back to the first of The Great 8 Virtues discussed in Chapter 3—Humility. Accountability is impossible without Humility. That's because our natural response is to get defensive when we receive criticism. But with Humility, we realize we're all vulnerable to Greed and need other people to help point out our blind spots.

2. Surround yourself with qualified people you can trust.

Who are the people you trust and respect, and who would be willing to hold you accountable? Seek them out. Spend consistent time with them. Invite them to hold your feet to the fire. Ask for their advice on overcoming the struggles you're confronting.

3. Follow through.

If you consistently ignore someone's feedback, they'll stop giving it. So, if you see merit in their recommendations, communicate how you will act on them—and follow through. And if, for any reason, you decide to go a different direction, explain your thinking. Invite them to "sanity check" your assumptions. Then, make your decision and execute.

Accountability at Scale: Achievement Updates

How do you instill Accountability throughout your company to counteract Greed?

Shift from a traditional performance review model to Achievement Updates. Think about it. After most performance reviews, employees think:

- *What was the point of that review?*

- *Honestly, I still have no idea how I'm doing.*

- *Why not tell me what I did wrong when I can do something to fix it—not several months later!*

Sound familiar?

Ever endured a "pointless" performance review in your career? But now you're the one in charge. How do you make your performance reviews count?

That's where Achievement Updates come in. They provide timely, consistent, and *valuable* feedback between owners, managers, and employees.

The problem is that most performance reviews fail for three reasons:

- **Poor alignment.** The employee's objectives are out of alignment with the company's goals. For example, a production manager has specific efficiency metrics to meet. But those numbers incentivize the employee to find ways to cut corners to hit the target. The manager is "successful," but the company suffers.

- **Broken feedback loop.** Far too many companies make performance reviews a once-a-year exercise. By the time the employee receives feedback, it's worthless.

- **Check-the-box mentality.** Performance management is often a check-the-box task for assigning pay raises or bonuses. This mentality overlooks what should be the purpose of performance reviews. And that's to connect with your team and coach them to perform at their best.

Fixing Performance Management

So, how do Achievement Updates fix the performance review process?

Follow these five guidelines for effective Achievement Updates:

1. Catch them "doing good."

Most performance reviews are either too vague or too negative. Fix both problems by focusing on specific positive results you want to reinforce. You might say, "Here's what I've seen you do that I appreciate and would love for you to keep doing."

Connect the dots for them. Talk about how their achievements are helping the company reach its goals. They will gain a greater sense of purpose in the company, motivating them to excel even higher.

2. Get *their* perspective.

Achievement Updates are conversations, not monologues. So, ask questions about how the person views priorities and performance. Then listen. Their answers will give you insight into what motivates them.

For example: "We've talked about your achievements I wanted to highlight. But I'm curious about your perspective. What do you see as your biggest accomplishments in the past 90 days? What makes you most excited about those wins? What are some of the lessons learned that you'd like to build upon in the next 90 days?"

3. Ask them to rate how they feel about their role.

Don't ask binary "yes or no" questions about their role. Even the most honest person will likely tell you what they think you want to hear.

Instead, give the employee more flexibility with a range question, such as "On a scale of 1 to 10, how do you feel about how your current role fits your personality, passion, and skills?"

If they give you any number less than 10, follow up with this question: "What would need to change to take that number to a 10?"

What if they say, "10"? Simple. Respond with this question: "If you could experience this role at an even higher level—say, an 11—what would need to change to reach that level?"

Their answers will give you the formula for setting them up for success—and keep them happy along the way.

4. Uncover the areas *they* want to improve.

It's human nature. If you point out something to an employee that you want them to improve, they'll see it as your problem. They'll work on it only if you stay on top of them.

But if you help them see the problem themselves, they will take ownership of it—and their plan to solve it.

How do you do that? Ask this question: "From your perspective, what have you struggled with the most in the past 90 days?" Then, continue the discussion with follow-up questions:

- "What do you think are the root causes of those challenges impeding your progress?"

- "What ideas come to mind for countering those issues over the next 90 days?"

- "Have you thought about [insert your recommendation]?"

- "What's your next step?"

Remember: You're not instructing them; you're *coaching* them.

5. Be timely and consistent.

Schedule Achievement Updates at least every 90 days. The shorter interval allows for more accurate and effective feedback.

Achievement Updates Keep Greed in Check

How do Achievement Updates counteract Greed in your company?

For one, you must check your Greed at the door before you can lead an effective Achievement Update. Every Achievement Update reminds you that you can only win if you help your team win.

Second, Achievement Updates create a culture of psychological safety that promotes collaboration. Otherwise, employees who feel unsafe will resort to greedy behavior to protect their interests.

The Bottom Line

Greed is a dark vice that works secretly, deep within our inner motivations. And we often don't know we've crossed the line from ambition to Greed until it's too late. But when we commit to Accountability, we can expose Greed, reduce its power, and establish a strong foundation for long-term success.

In the Trenches: The Pitfalls of No Accountability

Russ Clemmer

"I don't answer to anybody," was the reply from my boss, the pastor of my church, to a group of parents and boosters during the meeting.

I spent seven years teaching and coaching (and serving every other role I could grab) at a private school in South Carolina. The school was started by the church and grew to over 1,000 students. It was an excellent school known for its strong academics, arts, and sports.

But the sports programs mattered most to the pastor.

He approved the hire of "win-at-any-cost" coaches, pressured boosters into funding facilities beyond the program's needs, and ultimately lied to those who were supposed to hold him accountable.

He was a talented speaker, knew the Bible well, and appeared to be a wise counselor. But he surrounded himself with "yes men," enabling a culture of Greed.

Yet, the school was growing, the sports teams were winning, and the money was flowing.

Then, one day, he unilaterally approved a real estate transaction without proper oversight. This is the point when his house of cards began to crumble. He raised money for the sports facility expansion and improvement but spent it without clear communication with the donors.

When he was called into question, he blew everyone off.

It turns out that when wealthy people give money, they often expect a full report of how their donations were used to benefit the organization.

These donors and other parents demanded a meeting with him. He went to the meeting and attempted to smooth everything over with charm and intimidation. But he didn't anticipate the parents holding his feet to the fire. Someone asked him, "Who do you answer to?"

He replied smugly, "I don't answer to anybody."

Within six months of that meeting, the FBI got involved with the church and the school to investigate accusations of fraud. It turned out that both the pastor and the Head of School had diverted millions of dollars for their personal benefit. They both served prison time. And the church and school suffered the collateral damage of their Greed.

Virtuous leaders have since helped the church and the school rebuild the foundation of trust and excellence with the community and the families.

The lesson: The most dangerous perspective on Accountability is believing you can truly (and sustainably) succeed without it.

Deeper Reflection

1. You may not be Gordon Gekko. But we're all susceptible to Greed to some extent, whether we know it at the time or not. So, take time for reflection. What are some—perhaps subtle—ways that Greed has a grip on you?

2. Why? What about those areas in your life make you especially vulnerable to Greed?

3. To what extent has Greed undermined your leadership effectiveness?

4. What's at stake? What's the cost to you and your company if you don't keep the vice of Greed in check?

5. Who can you point to as an excellent role model for practicing Accountability? Who do they have in their circle to hold them accountable?

6. On a scale of 1 to 10, with 10 being the highest, how would you rate your level of Accountability? What would you need to change to move your rating from your current number to a 10?

7. What will it take for you and your company to shift from a performance reviews model to Achievement Updates?

8. What will be covered in your company's Achievement Updates?

9. How often will you schedule Achievement Updates?

10. Imagine you and your team practicing accountability at a high level. What would that look like? How would you describe the difference in your company? What would be the impact on your bottom line?

Remember:

When you commit to Accountability—to do the right thing, in the right way, with the right motives—you can shine a light on Greed, defuse its power, and put your company on a solid ethical foundation to achieve sustainable success.

CHAPTER 7:
VIRTUE #5: ACCEPTANCE VS. ANGER

"When a leader embraces their responsibility to care for people instead of caring for numbers, then people will follow, solve problems and see to it that that leader's vision comes to life the right way, a stable way and not the expedient way."

- Simon Sinek, Leaders Eat Last: Why Some Teams Pull Together and Others Don't

H e was dealt a lousy hand by any measure. But the legendary football coach Vince Lombardi didn't see it that way. He saw the potential to win if he could play his cards right.

And that's what he did.

In 1959, the Green Bay Packers hired the forty-five-year-old Lombardi as their new head coach and general manager. It was his first NFL head coaching job, and he had a daunting task. How do you turn around a franchise with more than 10 straight losing seasons?

Even worse, the Packers won only one game with ten losses the previous season when Lombardi took over.

But he didn't waste time raising expectations. "I have never been on a losing team, gentlemen, and I do not intend to start now," Lombardi said at the first team meeting.

His players got the message.

That first year, Lombardi guided the Packers to seven wins and five losses. It was the team's first winning season since 1947. And he did it with most of the players from the previous season. Lombardi would lead the Packers to five NFL Championships in nine years as head coach, including winning the first two Super Bowls in 1966-67.

During Lombardi's era in professional football, players didn't change teams like they do today in the NFL. For the most part, he had to work with the players he had. And that's what makes his transformation of the Packers so remarkable.

He didn't change the culture by changing the team's composition. He changed how the players thought about themselves and each other. As Packers.com put it: "Lombardi immediately changed the way the team looked, the way it played, and especially how it thought."

So, how did Lombardi win with a "losing" hand? How did he transform his team's thinking—and performance—so quickly?

He did many things well from a leadership perspective. However, one factor that stands out is that Lombardi demonstrated mastery over the vice of Anger.

Anger Distorts Your Vision

What does keeping Anger in check have to do with Lombardi's success?

You can imagine what it must have been like for Lombardi to step foot in a losing culture. Nobody likes change. And here he was to bring change. That causes friction.

Most of us would be tempted to get angry and resentful during such a clash of wills.

"Why did I get stuck with these guys? They're entitled, mentally soft, and have zero discipline! I'm being set up for failure!"

See what Anger does? It distorts your vision. You only see the negative in the other person or the situation, not the possibilities.

Lombardi saw the potential. And he trained his team to fulfill it.

Anger Defined

What is Anger?

Anger is the emotion that erupts when someone or something stands in the way of what you want.

In *Wooden on Leadership*, Hall of Fame basketball coach John Wooden writes, "A volatile leader is like a bottle of nitroglycerine: The slightest knock and it blows up. Those around nitroglycerine or a temperamental boss spend all their time carefully tiptoeing back and forth rather than doing their jobs. It is not an environment, in my opinion, conducive to a winning organization."

Have you ever worked for a boss like that? Did it make you dread going to work each day, not knowing what would set this person off?

A leader's uncontrolled Anger creates a chaotic, abusive, and drama-filled work environment. The team responds by focusing more on day-to-day self-preservation than working together toward a shared vision. In other words, Anger kills the Collaboration Effect on Profit.

"At least I would never be *that* boss!" you think to yourself.

But let's get real. We all have a breaking point. Perhaps it's one of these scenarios:

- A major deal that looked so promising yesterday is starting to unravel.

- An employee entrusted with much responsibility makes a critical and costly mistake.

- Sales are down, and you're feeling the heat from the Board or investors.

- A vendor "drops the ball" and jeopardizes a significant customer order.

- Things feel like they're falling apart at home, which spills over into your work and causes you to feel on edge.

In each scenario, our "default mode" as humans is to respond with Anger. We perceive that someone has gotten in the way of what we want. And we feel an irresistible urge to lash out at that person, which we see as the source of our problems.

Roman emperor and stoic philosopher Marcus Aurelius writes in *Meditations*, "How much more grievous are the consequences of anger than the causes of it."

Now, being angry isn't always bad. Occasionally displaying righteous indignation can be an effective way for a leader to communicate the need for urgency. When expressed appropriately, indignation can help grab attention and get people focused on the task.

But unbridled Anger will only lead to diminishing returns. It erodes trust, undermines team performance, and causes your most talented employees to leave.

Anger at Scale: Selfishness

What happens when Anger spreads beyond the owner to infect the entire team?

The result is the opposite of collaboration—selfishness.

If you follow professional sports, you've heard this saying: "Winning covers over a multitude of sins." As long as the team continues to win, the coach and teammates will tolerate each other's egos and idiosyncrasies.

But things begin to unravel when the team experiences adversity and starts losing. Their true character emerges. Tempers flare. Fingers point blame at one another. Trust breaks down. Each person looks only after themselves, and the organization suffers.

Fighting off Anger with Acceptance

How can you defuse the Anger inside you before it explodes?

Follow Coach Lombardi's lead. He practiced the virtue of Acceptance—the fifth of the Great 8 leadership virtues.

Acceptance puts you in a calm and resourceful mental state. You can see the potential in each team member despite their current performance. And you gain insight into where to put them in the company so they can flourish individually and as a team.

That's what Coach Lombardi did. He took the same players who lost all but one game the season before and quickly transformed them into perennial winners. By "accepting" his players as they were at that moment, he focused on looking for their unique giftedness. This way, he could put them in the best positions for the team to succeed. He then raised their expectations of themselves and held them accountable to live up to those expectations.

When we get angry, it's much like driving a vehicle mired in mud or sand. Out of frustration and anger, we naturally feel the urge to floor the proverbial gas pedal and accelerate ourselves out of the problem. But that makes the situation worse.

Now, suppose you're stuck, but you pause to assess the situation this time. Instead of trying to power your way out, you shift in reverse to move a few inches backward. Then you shift into drive to move forward a few inches. You repeat—rocking back and forth, back and forth—until you gain the traction you need to get unstuck.

That's what it looks like when practicing the virtue of Acceptance. When you encounter an issue, you resist the urge to punch the accelerator—to attack the person—out of Anger. Instead, you pause. You shift your mind into reverse to help you see and accept that person as a human being, not as an object of your wrath. And then, you gently work with that person to gain the "traction" you need to solve the problem.

Acceptance = Accepting the Person, Not the Problem

Before we go further, let's address some misconceptions about Acceptance. It does not mean:

- We accept someone's bad behavior or poor performance.
- We accept or agree with the other person's opinions.
- We accept someone's actions that harm us.

But it does mean we accept the person. In other words, Acceptance means separating the person from the problem.

Even in a culture of high Accountability, some people will fail to meet your expectations. But if you consider that people are more than obstacles or problems, you won't put them in the "I'm done with you!" category. This subtle mindset shift toward attacking the problem, not the person, goes a long way toward keeping Anger in check.

And that could save you a lot of heartache (and money) down the road. As Benjamin Franklin said, " Whatever begins in anger ends in shame."

Putting Acceptance into Practice

How can the virtue of Acceptance help you defuse Anger?

Here are three steps for putting Acceptance into daily practice:

1. Put yourself in an "accepting" frame of mind.

When you notice underperforming people on your team, how can you help them improve? Use this Acceptance Inventory to put you in the right mindset:

- Why did I hire them in the first place?
- What is causing them to underperform?
- What areas of giftedness do they bring to the table?
- How do they know when they are "on"—working in their sweet spot?
- Are they still a good fit for what we are trying to do?
- Are they open to being coached? Will they listen?
- What exactly do I want them to do now?
- Have I been clear in articulating my expectations?

These questions will help you see the possibilities in the person and discover the most effective course of action. You might determine the best thing for them and the company is to let them go. You have to be willing to face that reality.

But if you choose to keep them on the team, then "proclaim the truth in advance"–tell them about the giftedness you see in them and the actions they could take to improve their performance moving forward.

2. Remind them of the potential you see in them–and coach them to reach it.

You're working with an overzealous sales rep who makes unrealistic promises. And their behavior is damaging your company's reputation with customers. How do you address that behavior through Acceptance?

Review the Acceptance Inventory questions above. Then meet with that individual and say something along these lines:

"Remember the reason you came on board with us? You love being with people and can develop long-term and loyal customer relationships. But the high-pressure approach you're taking right now is pushing customers away. Take your time with the customer. Ask discovery questions like these to help you uncover the ideal solution for the customer and us. If you do that, you could take your sales and income to a new level."

Then, work with that rep after each discovery call to debrief: What went well? What's the next step? What could they improve for next time?

3. Show, don't tell.

One of the biggest mistakes coaches make in sports is that they talk too much. They give too much verbal instruction with too little demonstration and constructive feedback.

You see the same thing in business. If you want to change someone's behavior and performance, don't just talk about it. Work alongside them and demonstrate what it takes to succeed while offering helpful feedback to help them learn, grow, and thrive.

Acceptance at Scale: Personality & Leadership Style Assessments

How do you instill Acceptance throughout your company to counteract Anger?

That's where Personality and Leadership Style Assessments come in. Tools such as Myers-Briggs, DiSC Profile, and Enneagram can equip you and your team with a shared vocabulary for discussing each other's differences. They offer insights into how to listen and speak to one another based on awareness of each other's strengths and personalities.

That's because each team member is unique in personality and leadership style. Teams that understand each other have the best opportunity to succeed together. By promoting the virtue of Acceptance, you can accept those around you for who they are, creating a healthy culture.

The assessments help you and your team reflect on each other's communication preferences, make decisions, and resolve conflict. Where do similarities between teammates make them work better together than apart? When do the similarities cause friction? Where do their differences lead to better collaboration? When could those differences create conflict?

But beware of the temptation of using assessment results *against* people, especially in these two ways:

- **Labeling and limiting them:** "They're an introvert. They wouldn't be good at sales."

- **Patronizing them:** "You're a high S and C, and that's why you don't [fill in the blank]."

Instead, use your understanding of your team's similarities and differences to "accept" who they are (and want to become). This way, you gain a clearer insight into where to put them in the best positions to succeed.

The Bottom Line

Coach Wooden said, "My teaching stressed that 'losing your temper will get us outplayed because you'll make unnecessary errors; your judgment will be impaired.' I didn't mind an occasional mistake unless it was caused by loss of self-control."

We're vulnerable to Anger when people don't perform or behave to our expectations. And when we lose control of our anger, our natural response is to confront the problem by attacking the person involved.

But the virtue of Acceptance offers us a more productive way to address an issue by causing us to pause and reflect on the humanity of those who have fallen short of our expectations.

The result: We make thoughtful, measured decisions that serve the company's best interests. And we create a "safe place" for our people to work and collaborate to achieve success.

In the Trenches: Proclaiming the Truth in Advance

David Harper

In our book, *Light Their Fire for God*, my wife Anne tells a story about when she was a high school teacher. She had an incorrigible student, Johnny (not his real name), who was being as disruptive as he could be–walking on tables, pulling students' chairs out from under them, yelling obnoxious comments, and disrupting the class at any given moment.

Anne writes, "As Johnny and I stood in the hall alone, I looked him in the eyes and said, 'Johnny, I just want you to know how glad I am that you are in my class. People look up to you, and you have the potential of being a great leader. I think you have many wonderful qualities. We are going to have a great time here, and I am happy to have you in my class. All right, you can go back in now.' At the risk of sounding melodramatic, Johnny went back into that class a different boy. Without further correction, he stopped climbing on the furniture, yelling for attention, and disrupting any other students. Furthermore, he would frequently come to my desk and ask, 'Mrs. Harper, is there anything I can do to help you?'"

In that hallway with Johnny, Anne modeled **the virtue of Acceptance** by practicing a principle we now call "**Proclaiming the Truth in Advance**." It's the idea of envisioning the best possibilities of what could be and calling the person into that reality. **You *accept* the situation and the person, meet them where they are, and then help them see a preferred vision for their future.**

Here are some other examples:

Situation: Our three-year-old son, Daniel, wasn't staying in bed when we put him down. I wanted to get angry and punish him again. That would have been the easy way out.

- **Proclaiming the Truth in Advance:** My wife Anne had a better idea. She said, "Isn't Daniel the most obedient child!" That caught my attention, and I joined in with her saying the same thing. We were stating the truth about him in advance of it happening. The next morning, he woke up believing he was "the most obedient child."

Situation: I was coaching football at a high school that had not thought about winning their conference, let alone a state title.

- **Proclaiming the Truth in Advance:** Before our first game of the season, the boys wanted to camp out on the field the night before the last day of two-a-day practices. That night, we placed a lantern in the middle of our semicircle and looked toward the stadium, saying, "Wow, can you imagine what this stadium would look like if we could return to the glory days?" That year, we won the state championship in that stadium!

Situation: "Working with these guys is like 'herding butterflies!'"

- **Proclaiming the Truth in Advance:** "Let's stay the course. One of these days, we will look back and see a great story unfold better than we could ever have imagined." And we're seeing it happen!

Now, does "proclaiming the truth in advance" always work? Of course not! And it doesn't mean you delude yourself and insincerely flatter the other person. **You have to genuinely see the possibilities in them.** But I think you'll agree that "proclaiming the truth in advance" is a much more effective *starting point* in influencing behavior than lashing out or giving up.

Deeper Reflection

1. We're all vulnerable to Anger. Sometimes, you're able to hold your cool longer than other times. It depends on the trigger. So, take time for reflection. What are some situations that trigger you to have angry outbursts?

2. Why? What about those scenarios in your life cause you to be especially susceptible to Anger?

3. To what extent has Anger undermined your leadership effectiveness?

4. What's at stake? What's the cost to you and your company if you don't keep the vice of Anger in check?

5. Who can you point to as an excellent role model for practicing Acceptance? What are specific ways they exhibit Acceptance?

6. On a scale of 1 to 10, with 10 being the highest, how would you rate your level of Acceptance? What would you need to change to move your rating from your current number to a 10?

7. What systems does the company have to identify, discuss, and accommodate differences in leadership styles and personalities?

8. How do you avoid misusing personality assessments in a way that pigeonholes or patronizes employees?

9. When and how often will you schedule personality assessments?

10. Imagine you and your team practicing Acceptance at a high level. What would that look like? How would you describe the difference in your company? What would be the impact on your bottom line?

> **Remember:**
>
> *Diffuse Anger with Acceptance. Take a step back when things aren't going your way. Make allowances for people who appear to be your obstacles. And then, with an open mind and calm heart, consider all the possible options to help you move the situation and the relationship forward.*

CHAPTER 8:
VIRTUE #6: INTEGRITY VS. DISHONESTY

"A good name is more desirable than great riches; to be esteemed is better than silver or gold."
- Proverbs 22:1

Many praised his decision. Others couldn't understand it. But it was business as usual for the former world number one tennis player, Andy Roddick.

On May 5, 2005, Roddick, an American, played Fernando Verdasco of Spain in the round of 16 at the Italia Masters tennis tournament in Rome, Italy. Roddick was the top seed in the tournament, heavily favored to win the match and advance to the next round.

As expected, Roddick dominated the match and was about to win when something unusual happened.

COLLABORATION EFFECT ON PROFIT

After Verdasco appeared to hit his second serve just long, the line judge called the serve out and awarded Roddick the point and the match.

Verdasco ran to the net to congratulate the American on his victory. But Roddick did the unthinkable. He refused to accept the winning call. He pointed to the mark on the clay where Verdasco's serve had hit to prove it was in. The official overturned the call and awarded the point to Verdasco.

The Spaniard made the most of his second chance to come back and win the game, set, and match.

Integrity cost Roddick the match and tens of thousands of dollars in prize money. But he didn't dwell on what he lost. Nor did he bask in the worldwide praise for his exceptional sportsmanship.

"I didn't think it was anything extraordinary," Roddick said. "The umpire would have done the same thing if he came down and looked."

The Pressure to Compromise

But it *was* extraordinary. How many of us would have spoken up if we were in Andy Roddick's shoes?

We'd all like to think we'd do the right thing. But it wouldn't be without feeling the intense pressure to stay quiet.

- *"The call is the call—it's not my fault if the officials get it wrong."*

- *"I have a family to provide for."*

- *"I have a reputation and record to protect."*

The reality is that the vice of Dishonesty is not only about telling outright lies. It's also about staying quiet when we should speak up and correct the record. And it's about compromising the truth on the apparent "little things."

For example, you might be tempted to:

- Withhold candid feedback to a client out of fear of angering—and losing—a customer representing a large chunk of the business.

- Steer customers toward products most profitable to you but unsuitable for the client.

- "Get creative" with the books to make the company's numbers look more attractive to a potential buyer.

In these moments, you feel pressured to rationalize and compromise your standards. But if you relent, you set a precedent for your team that honesty is only the best policy when it doesn't cost too much.

Dishonesty Defined

What is Dishonesty?

It's lying or withholding the truth to protect one's reputation or manipulate the other party to respond in one's favor.

Andy Roddick paid a high price for telling the truth. But keeping quiet would have been much more costly for him in the long run.

As Dan Ariely writes in *The Honest Truth About Dishonesty: How We Lie to Everyone - Especially Ourselves*: "When we and those around us are dishonest, we start suspecting everyone, and without trust, our lives become more difficult in almost every way."

If Dishonesty shapes our decisions, things break down. We're no longer "whole." We become two selves. One is consistent with truth; the other struggles to reconcile the truth with our actions.

Dishonesty at Scale: Misaligned Incentives

What happens when Dishonesty spreads beyond the owner to infect the entire team?

You get something akin to the Wells Fargo fake account scandal in the 2010s.

Bank executives pressured rank-and-file employees to meet unrealistic sales quotas. This led to employees opening millions of new accounts for customers without their knowledge or approval.

The scandal would cost the bank $3 billion in 2020 to settle probes into its fraudulent sales practices. But it cost much more than that. It created a culture of Dishonesty that rewarded employees for cheating customers.

Wells Fargo management did nothing to stop the fraud—in fact, they tried to cover it up—until the news broke in 2016.

The lesson: When left unchecked, Dishonesty will corrupt the entire company. "The more people rationalize cheating, the more it becomes a culture of dishonesty," Stephen Covey said. "And that can become a vicious, downward cycle. Because suddenly, if everyone else is cheating, you feel a need to cheat, too."

Once the cheating cycle begins, it becomes too hard to stop. And that's the big lesson from the Wells Fargo scandal: Beware of the behaviors you reward.

Fighting off Dishonesty with Integrity

How can you resist the temptation to shade the truth when under pressure?

Practice Integrity, the sixth of the Great 8 Virtues. What exactly does Integrity mean?

The English word for Integrity comes from the Latin *integer*, meaning "wholeness, completeness." So, think of Integrity as the virtue of "being whole" based on consistency of character.

As serial entrepreneur and angel investor Naval Ravikant defines it: "Integrity is when what you think and what you say and what you do are one."

Integrity is the most valuable currency in the marketplace. It builds trust with customers, employees, investors, and other stakeholders. And that trust becomes the unshakable foundation for your company's long-term success.

If you breach that trust, you put those relationships—and your entire business—at risk.

Integrity = Transparency, Not Perfection

Before we go further, let's address a myth about Integrity. It does *not* mean perfection. In fact, a healthy Integrity practice begins by admitting you don't have perfect Integrity. None of us do.

We've all succumbed to Dishonesty with others—and ourselves. And we'll continue to do so at some level while on this planet. Dishonesty is ingrained in human nature, flaring up when we feel threatened, embarrassed, and insecure.

But when we're in tune with Integrity, we understand we'll make mistakes. We'll fail to live up to our word. But when we do, Integrity counteracts our natural urge to lie to cover things up. Instead, it guides us to be transparent, accept full responsibility, and earn back the trust of those we hurt.

Putting Integrity into Practice

How can you blunt the influence of Dishonesty on your decision-making?

Follow these five steps for putting Integrity into daily practice:

1. Get honest with yourself.

We're human. We all make poor decisions, including ones where we play fast and loose with the truth. But when you recognize what you've done, come clean, outline a plan to correct the issue, and take action.

2. Set up an early warning system.

Ask people you trust to hold you accountable for Integrity. This way, you have an "early warning system." It alerts you to any discrepancies between your values and actions. And you can counteract Dishonesty before it damages your company's reputation.

As Thomas Paine said, "Character is much easier kept than recovered."

3. Remove the pressure points.

Want to avoid the temptation to compromise your ethics?

Improve how you run your business. For example, suppose one customer has become too large a percentage of your profits. Now, you feel pressure to do whatever it takes to keep the account. And that includes tolerating unethical behavior from yourself, the client, and your team.

So, review your business processes and systems. Where are your vulnerabilities—your most sensitive pressure points? What systems can you improve to solve those issues before they put you in a bad spot?

4. Over-communicate.

When you have bad news for someone, don't sit on it. Be candid about the problem and willing to work with them on a solution so they know you have their back.

5. Be known for follow-through.

This step is an obvious point. But how often have you been around charismatic leaders who can win you over with their big ideas but fail to deliver? They're great at starting things but can't seem ever to finish.

Eventually, you stop believing in them—that they have the discipline or even the skill to get the job done.

When you follow through on commitments, you earn the trust of your stakeholders. And they will listen to—and act upon—your ideas because you've built up your "currency" of credibility with them.

Integrity at Scale: High-Trust Communication

How do you instill the practice of Integrity throughout your company?

Model, teach, and incentivize High-Trust Communication at all company levels.

What is High-Trust Communication? It's being transparent and candid with others—especially when delivering unpleasant news.

Consider this story.

A business owner—we'll call him James—approaches retirement age. He wants to sell the business but won't tell his team, fearful they'll leave the company before he can close a deal.

James doesn't realize that his employees already suspect he's looking to sell. After all, he's not getting any younger and hasn't groomed anyone internally to become the next CEO.

Eventually, James' fear of being transparent with his team becomes a self-fulfilling prophecy. His top people jump ship, losing trust in their boss and the company's future.

The very thing he feared he caused to happen because he refused to be candid with his team.

As leaders, we've all been in similar situations. We're tempted to withhold information that we believe could harm us.

But this is the vice of Dishonesty at work. And, far too often, it produces the outcomes we want to avoid.

If you were in James' position, how would you apply High-Trust Communication? Consider your audience and what they can handle—and what they need to know to do their jobs well. Some things you'll be able to share, and some you can't say due to legal or other reasons.

So, what should you say to establish trust with your team? Follow these four High-Trust Communication principles:

1. Connect with your audience.

Begin by addressing the elephant in the room—what you know is on their minds.

"You have probably already been thinking about this: What is our company's future? Will I sell? Will I bring someone in to take over? What will be the impact on your jobs?"

2. Speak with candor.

Label the emotions you believe they're feeling at that moment. Then shoot straight with them. Don't try to set them at ease by telling them what they want to hear. Anything short of the unvarnished truth will undercut your credibility.

"I understand the anxiety that this uncertainty may cause you to feel. And I don't have all the answers for you right now."

3. Show them respect.

You're not in a position to tell them all the details. But make them feel respected by telling them what you can say.

"But here's what I can tell you. I am exploring different opportunities to transition out of the company. We've built

something special together, and I want to ensure I leave this company and you in good hands. And as things become clearer, I'll keep you posted on what you can expect."

4. Lead them to action or a solution.

Send them off on an action-oriented note.

"In the meantime, we're full steam ahead doing what we do best in serving our customers."

Whatever you do, be clear and to the point. Otherwise, you risk losing the other party's attention—and trust. As the author and psychologist Celia Green said, "Lack of clarity is always a sign of dishonesty."

Case Study: Jeff Weiner, Former LinkedIn CEO

Former LinkedIn CEO Jeff Weiner delivered a master class in High-Trust Communication in his letter to employees after the company announced its acquisition by Microsoft in June 2016.

(Read Weiner's full letter here: https://www.linkedin.com/pulse/linkedin-microsoft-changing-way-world-works-jeff-weiner/.)

You can imagine the uncertainty his team faced at the time. How will the acquisition affect their future? How will it change their jobs right now? Weiner addressed the elephant in the room:

Now, onto the most crucial question: What does this mean for you specifically as an employee of LinkedIn?

> *Given our ability to operate independently, little is expected to change: You'll have the same title, the same manager, and the same role you currently have. The one exception: For those members of the team whose jobs are entirely focused on maintaining LinkedIn's status as a publicly traded company, we'll be helping you find your next play. In terms of everything else, it should be business as usual. We have the same mission and vision; we have the same culture and values; and I'm still the CEO of LinkedIn.*

Weiner anticipated his employees' concerns and addressed them head-on. He was candid about how some employees' roles would be eliminated. But he showed them respect throughout the letter. And he led them to action, saying LinkedIn would work alongside them, "helping you find your next play."

The Bottom Line

It's easy to keep your Integrity intact when things are going well. But what about when you feel pressure to stretch the truth or conceal it because honesty is too costly?

Look at Andy Roddick's example. Integrity's short-term pain pales compared to a reputation as someone people can trust under any circumstance.

As the Hebrew Proverb says, "A good name is more desirable than great riches; to be esteemed is better than silver or gold."

In the Trenches: Resisting the Urge to Justify

David Harper

A few years ago, we had our annual leadership team planning meeting at our home. My wife Anne doesn't typically participate, but she does listen to what's going on when she's around.

During one session, I described how I tried selling a client on a concept. But Anne couldn't hold herself back. She said, "I hate to say this, but you sound more like you're selling rather than serving."

She was saying that I put my own self-interest ahead of the client. And I was unwittingly about to cross the line into Dishonesty if I didn't pull myself back.

Why tell this story?

Before we, as the Legacy team, started being intentional about practicing The Great 8 Virtues, I would have immediately gotten defensive and perhaps angry about Anne's comments.

But at that moment, I became more open to her words. And that's a good thing because I knew Anne was right the more I thought about it!

In Hunter Lambeth's book, *Praus: A Parable for Winning the War Within* (the companion book to *The Great 8*), the protagonist, Jack, is listening to the mystical older version of himself who says, "You see, Dishonesty perpetuates itself because the world somehow convinces us that it's justified. We learn this from an early age, and then the belief gains momentum as we get older. We call others out on it but don't recognize the same behavior in ourselves. In some ways it's nothing more than practiced denial. We find justification for any action, no matter how dishonest it might be."

The reality is that none of us are perfect. We all violate our own principles from time to time, engaging in dishonest behavior and justifying it afterward. But you can break the cycle with these three critical takeaways:

1. Surround yourself with people you trust to "give it to you straight" (and listen to them).

2. Resist the urge to get defensive and justify.

3. Be intentional about practicing The Great 8 Virtues—including Integrity—to increase your sensitivity to the threat of potential incursions by the vices.

Deeper Reflection

1. We're most susceptible to Dishonesty when we're under pressure. So, take time for reflection. What situations have caused you to withhold or cover up the truth?

2. Why? What about those scenarios make you especially vulnerable to acting dishonestly?

3. To what extent has Dishonesty undermined your leadership effectiveness?

4. What's at stake? What's the cost to you and your company if you don't keep the vice of Dishonesty in check?

5. Who can you point to as an excellent role model for practicing Integrity? What traits do you see in them that demonstrate their Integrity?

6. On a scale of 1 to 10, with 10 being the highest, how would you rate your level of Integrity? What would you need to change to move your rating from your current number to a 10?

7. Reflect on the Wells Fargo scandal. What does your company incentivize—Integrity or Dishonesty?

8. What adjustments should your company make to its incentive structure to ensure you encourage the desired behavior?

9. How can you and your leadership team promote High-Trust Communication throughout the company?

10. Imagine you and your team practicing integrity at a high level. What would that look like? How would you describe the difference in your company? What would be the impact on your bottom line?

Remember:

Most companies place Integrity at the top of their corporate values. But Integrity can't just be a core value posted on the wall. It must be a virtue that you and your team practice day in and day out. Otherwise, the pressure to compromise Integrity for short-term gains will become too strong to resist.

CHAPTER 9:
VIRTUE #7: PEACEMAKING VS. TERRITORIALISM

> *"Peace is not absence of conflict; it is the ability to handle conflict by peaceful means."*
> - **Ronald Reagan**

For almost 50 years, Eric Lomax's hatred for Nagase Takashi consumed his every thought. But what happens when the victim and tormentor face each other again decades later?

It's not what you'd expect.

In 1942, the Japanese captured Lomax, a 19-year-old British soldier, during World War II. They took him to Thailand as slave labor to work on the Death Railway, a railroad between Thailand and Burma.

During his three-and-a-half years of imprisonment, Lomax experienced brutal torture. His captors waterboarded, starved, and beat him until they broke several bones.

His primary torturer? Nagase Takashi, a Japanese soldier who also served as an interpreter.

Lomax was finally freed in 1945 after the Japanese surrender. But he struggled to reintegrate into civilian life. He felt consumed by hatred towards Takashi and haunted by the memories of his torture.

Meanwhile, Takashi didn't face charges of war crimes. He claimed he was only an interpreter and didn't torture anyone.

Four decades later, Lomax decided to investigate the events around his captivity. His goal was clear: Find Takashi and get revenge. Eye for an eye. Bone for a bone. He wanted Takashi to feel the same pain he felt.

But something happened that changed his mind. He found an article about Takashi feeling devastated by guilt over his treatment of one particular British soldier.

It dawned on Lomax: *He* was that soldier. And for the first time, he became open to forgiving his nemesis.

After corresponding back and forth, the two men agreed to meet in Thailand in 1993. That day, they embraced with tears streaming as they let go of decades of hatred and animosity and became the most unlikely of friends.

The walls of Territorialism, which once separated the two men, came crashing down.

Tearing Down the Walls

"When we met, Nagase greeted me with a formal bow," Lomax said on the Forgiveness Project (https://www.

theforgivenessproject.com/), a British website that publishes stories from survivors and perpetrators of crime and conflict who have rebuilt their lives. "I took his hand and said in Japanese, 'Good morning, Mr. Nagase, how are you?' He was trembling and crying, and he said over and over again: 'I am so sorry, so very sorry.' "

Lomax realized Nagase had also suffered—tormented by decades of relentless remorse.

"I had come with no sympathy for this man, and yet Nagase, through his complete humility, turned this around," Lomax said. "In the days that followed, we spent a lot of time together, talking and laughing."

The lesson of the story? Despite being out of prison for decades, Lomax still wasn't free. But that changed when he stood face-to-face with his enemy, ready to tear down the walls between them. That's when both men became free. Lomax, from hatred. Takashi, from guilt.

Now, most of us have never been prisoners of war. But we've all experienced Territorialism.

How?

Think about it:

- Do you ever hold grudges you can't let go of?
- Do you ever feel threatened by someone else's success?
- Do you ever view life or business through the lens of us vs. them?

If you answered Yes to any of these scenarios, you've tasted Territorialism. And if you allow this vice to fester and build momentum within you, it will crush everything you care about.

Territorialism Defined

What is Territorialism?

Territorialism sees another person or group as "the other," an enemy who wants to take you down and take what's yours. And it's the wall that pits people and departments against each other. They work in silos, competing for resources and recognition, each person for themself.

Territorialism compels you to view the world through a zero-sum lens. If they win, you lose. So, you do everything possible to prevent them from winning.

But here's the uncomfortable truth: Territorialism is our "default mode." Our instinct is to act in ways that preserve our power and position. But that impulse will get us into trouble if we don't learn how to override it.

Territorialism at Scale: Team Dysfunction

What happens when Territorialism spreads beyond the owner to infect the entire team?

Teamwork breaks down. The silo effect emerges. Departments stop collaborating. And you start seeing:

- Senior leaders refuse to hire superstars who might outshine them.
- Middle managers obsess about political posturing and setting up rivals for failure.

- Frontline workers undermine their colleagues who threaten their status in the company.

As Territorialism grabs hold of the culture, you see a lot of sniping, complaining, and sabotaging. The next thing you know, your company stops growing because everyone is rowing in different directions.

Fighting off Territorialism with Peacemaking

How can you tear down the walls of Territorialism to build a high-performance culture?

Practice Peacemaking, the seventh of the Great 8 Virtues.

Territorialism is about scarcity–fear of loss. It causes people to get defensive and protect their turf at all costs. It sees business as a zero-sum game: "For me to win, I must make sure you lose."

But Peacemaking takes on an abundance mindset. It says, "If you and I can resolve our differences and work together, we both can win–and on a much bigger scale than either of us could achieve alone."

Peacemaking = Facing the Fight

Before we go further, let's address a common misconception about Peacemaking.

Conventional wisdom says that Peacemaking means avoiding conflict, as described by these thoughts:

- *I don't want to rock the boat right now.*
- *We can't afford to offend and lose our biggest client.*

- *I don't want to run off our star employee.*

But, Peacemaking is about strength, not weakness. If you avoid uncomfortable conversations to "keep the peace," you're not practicing Peacemaking. You're setting the stage for much worse conflict later.

Putting Peacemaking into Practice

How can you confront—and defeat—Territorialism within yourself?

Follow these five steps for putting Peacemaking into daily practice:

1. Invite candid conversations.

Peacemakers surround themselves with a "team of rivals" who challenge their thinking. They're not afraid of confrontation or dissenting opinions. Instead, they invite candid conversations. That's because they understand that allowing healthy disagreements creates a high-trust culture where collaboration can flourish.

2. Take responsibility.

Ask yourself, "What role might I have played in causing the situation? Did I say or do anything that could have set the conflict in motion or escalated it? Think about your contribution to the conflict. When you consider the other side, you're in a better position to work through the disagreement.

3. See the possibilities.

Albert Einstein once said, "In the middle of difficulty lies opportunity." You can say the same thing about conflict.

Breakthrough ideas and stronger relationships often emerge from the friction created by well-managed disagreements.

4. Think win-win.

Mary Parker Follett, a pioneer in organizational theory and behavior, said, "There are three ways of dealing with difference: domination, compromise, and integration. By domination, only one side gets what it wants; by compromise, neither side gets what it wants; by integration, we find a way by which both sides may get what they wish."

Think about the concerns and interests of the other party. Then, look for the common ground. This way, you can generate ideas that lead to a resolution both sides can embrace.

5. Clear the air.

Avoid the temptation to engage in passive-aggressive behavior. And don't let the issue fester. Talk to the person as soon as possible. As President Reagan said, "I've always believed that a lot of the troubles in the world would disappear if we were talking to each other instead of about each other."

Peacemaking at Scale: Healthy Conflict Management

How do you instill the practice of Peacemaking throughout your company?

Promote, manage, and resolve conflict in a healthy way.

In *Up the Organization: How to Stop the Corporation from Stifling People and Strangling Profits*, Robert Townsend writes, "A good manager doesn't try to eliminate conflict; he tries to keep it from wasting the energies of his people. If you're the boss and your people fight you openly when they think you are wrong—that's healthy."

Townsend makes an important point: As the boss, stop trying to prevent conflict. Don't push everyone to "be positive" or dismiss dissenters as "negative influences." Otherwise, people will default to keeping their disagreements to themselves. Instead of eliminating conflict, you will have only suppressed it.

What Does Healthy Conflict Management Look Like?

Go directly to the person and follow these four steps:

Step 1: Take the initiative.

Pat, do you have a few minutes? Can we talk?

Refrain from conversing via text or email, where things can be misunderstood. Instead, talk face-to-face or, at least, on the phone. This way, each of you can receive "live" feedback to make the discussion more productive.

Step 2: Understand the other person's perspective.

When you first came on board, you seemed excited about your work. And it showed in your performance. But lately, you haven't been yourself. How are things going for you? From your perspective, what do you think has changed?

Resist any urge to either defend yourself or interject with snap solutions. Just listen. The idea here is to invite the other person to be authentic with you. You want them to feel safe to speak about whatever they're thinking without judgment.

Step 3: Confirm your understanding.

You feel that … [reflect on your understanding of what that person told you]. Is that accurate?"

Again, listen. Ask questions to clarify anything you might have misunderstood until they say, "Yes, that's it."

Step 4: Share your perspective.

"I hear where you're coming from. And I can understand why you might feel that way. Here's where I'm coming from, and hopefully, this can help shed some light on how we can work through this together."

At this point, the other person feels respected and heard. Now, they're ready to open up and listen to what you have to say.

What If the Direct Approach Doesn't Help?

In most conflicts, both sides have contributed to the problem to some degree. So, find someone you both trust to serve as a referee. They can help set and enforce ground rules that allow a "safe place" for the parties to have an open conversation.

Your goal is to understand where the other person is coming from—and for them to understand you. This sets the stage for resolution, forgiveness, and a stronger relationship.

What If Things Don't Work Out?

Healthy Conflict Management won't always lead to a happy ending. After all, you might decide during that meeting to let the employee go in the best interest of both parties. But, at least you showed them respect. You listened to them and addressed the situation before it worsened.

The Bottom Line

Peacemaking is hard work. And it takes a great deal of vulnerability to restore broken relationships. But the payoff is enormous.

Look at Eric Lomax and Nagase Takashi. Their reconciliation is a model for the world of what true Peacemaking looks like. Think about all those decades of life they lost, wallowing in anger and guilt. But with their embrace in 1993, they broke free from the past and began living again.

What has the vice of Territorialism taken from you? Begin today to put Peacemaking into practice to restore the broken relationships in your life, family, and business.

In the Trenches: Shifting from Territorial to Collaborative

David Harper

One day in 2017, Russ and I were about to meet with the attorney to sign legal documents for our long-term transition plan. Unfortunately, we hadn't yet "discovered" **The 3 Wins Framework** (Chapters 11-15), which would have helped us structure a better plan upfront. So, what happens next shouldn't be a surprise.

Russ called me that morning and said, "We need to reschedule. I'm not comfortable with how we're calculating the value of the company."

My reaction wasn't good. We had been working on this plan for about six months. I started feeling angry and territorial. I was thinking, "We agreed and should hold to it! He just doesn't get it! What's wrong with him? We're getting this done!"

Then it dawned on me, "Wait a minute! If Russ isn't completely comfortable with this, how could I ever expect it to work out well if we go through with it?"

By then, we had started practicing The Great 8 Virtues at Legacy. I knew I needed to overcome my negative emotions by demonstrating the virtues—like Humility, Empathy, and Peacemaking—to understand Russ' concerns.

I called him back and said, "Russ, thank you for having the courage to stick by your guns on this issue. You absolutely did the right thing here."

That *instantly* changed our dynamic around this issue— from territorial to collaborative.

We agreed to spend more time with a valuation professional to help us get it right. And within a few weeks, we arrived at an agreement that, ultimately, worked out better for both of us.

Without Russ and I being committed to living The Great 8 Virtues, I don't know whether we could have resolved this issue productively—or at all—without a lot of hurt and resentment.

Deeper Reflection

1. Reflect on the Lomax-Takashi story. Do you hold a grudge you can't let go of?

2. If yes, what would it take for you to forgive that person?

3. Now, take the flip side: Have *you* hurt someone deeply and never apologized?

4. What steps could you take to reconcile that relationship?

5. To what extent has Territorialism undermined your leadership effectiveness?

6. What's at stake? What's the cost to you and your company if you don't keep the vice of Territorialism in check?

7. Who can you point to as an excellent role model for practicing Peacemaking? What traits do you see in them that show their ability to manage conflict well?

8. On a scale of 1 to 10, with 10 being the highest, how would you rate your level of putting Peacemaking into daily practice? What would you need to change to move your rating from your current number to a 10?

9. How can you and your leadership team instill Healthy Conflict Management throughout the company?

10. Imagine you and your team practicing peacemaking at a high level. What would that look like? How would you describe the difference in your company? What would be the impact on your bottom line?

> **Remember:**
>
> *No matter how aligned your team might be, the reality is that conflict is inevitable. The key is learning how to manage those disagreements constructively.*

CHAPTER 10:
VIRTUE #8: COURAGE VS. FEAR

"Courage is the most important of all the virtues because, without courage, you can't practice any other virtue consistently."
- Maya Angelou

I t was the summer of 1940, and Western Civilization hung in the balance.

The Nazis steamrolled through France, capturing the nation in less than six weeks. Now, Adolph Hitler eyed an invasion of Great Britain, the last obstacle to Germany's complete control of Western Europe.

This was the backdrop for Prime Minister Winston Churchill's "Finest Hour" speech to the House of Commons on June 18, 1940, which would become one of the most consequential speeches ever delivered.

The stakes were never higher. Could Britain withstand the fast and furious Nazi Blitzkrieg coming their way? Or would their defenses, like the French's, get so overwhelmed they'd have to give up?

Churchill's speech was defiant, rallying the British around this bold vision:

> Let us, therefore, brace ourselves to our duties, and so bear ourselves that, if the British Empire and its Commonwealth last for a thousand years, men will still say, "This was their finest hour."

You know how the story ends. It was, indeed, Britain's finest hour. And the Allies would go on to defeat the Nazis five years later.

The Fine Line Between Wisdom and Fear

But things could have ended much differently.

As the Nazis swept through France, Winston Churchill was embroiled in a battle at home. Historians call it the "1940 British War Cabinet Crisis."

Leading the resistance against Churchill was Lord Halifax, his foreign secretary. Halifax proposed that Churchill should seek peace with Germany before France surrendered. He argued that Britain could keep its freedom by making concessions, like sacrificing a few former German colonies and accepting Nazi dominance over central Europe.

But Churchill disagreed. He argued that a premature peace would yield worse terms than resistance. And he had no faith in the Nazi regime's promises, saying that peace guaranteed by Hitler was no real peace.

Fortunately, Churchill won over the War Cabinet. But the debate reveals something interesting about the vice of Fear.

It's often disguised as positive traits—like prudence, wisdom, and "being realistic."

You can imagine Halifax thinking, "Look! Let's get real here! The Nazis steamrolled the French. We barely evacuated Dunkirk in time. And now we want to provoke an invasion of Britain? Let's not be stupid! Let's negotiate from a position of strength before our necks get crushed under Hitler's boot."

Sounds reasonable. But Halifax saw only one possible outcome from war with Germany—his country's defeat.

That's when you know the vice of Fear has a grip on you. It narrows your field of vision. It impairs your ability to consider all of the available options. What you believe to be the most prudent choice is the only one you can see.

In contrast, Churchill could see the entire field, with a much wider range of options. He considered the impact of surrender on the citizens' morale. If the British leadership gave up, would the people lose hope? And besides, how would it be wise to trust any peace agreement with Hitler?

For Churchill, Halifax's preemptive peace plan would lead to defeat by default. It would sentence the British to a future of brutal Nazi rule.

No. Fear would not prevail. Britain would choose to fight. And fight to win and protect its freedom and soul.

Fear Defined

What is Fear?

On the one hand, Fear is a natural emotion triggered by a perceived threat or danger. It can be a valuable tool for keeping us safe and helping us to make good decisions in dangerous situations. But when it's excessive or irrational, it's no longer helpful. It morphs into a destructive vice.

For example, your biggest client abuses your employees, creating a toxic work environment. How do you respond?

The right thing to do is talk with the client to resolve the issue. But the so-called voice of wisdom says, "Let's slow down here. We don't want to anger this customer and risk losing the account. Let's give it some time and see if things work themselves out."

Yet, if you let it go, your employees will assume you don't have their back—that you don't care about them. This belief will crush your team's morale and productivity.

Doing the right thing can be scary, especially with high stakes. But allowing Fear to cause you to do something you regret? Now, *that* should terrify you much, much more.

Fear at Scale: Toxic Culture

What happens when Fear spreads beyond the owner to infect the entire team?

Fear creates a toxic culture that leads to:

- **Low trust:** Employees become more focused on self-preservation and less willing to collaborate.

- **Low morale:** Employees feel stressed, anxious, and demotivated, leading to decreased productivity and a lack of commitment.

- **Less innovation:** Employees are afraid of making mistakes. And they're less willing to take risks or suggest new ideas, stifling creativity.

Fighting off Fear with Courage

So, how can you win the battle over Fear?

Practice Courage, the last—and perhaps the most important—of the Great 8 Virtues. As C.S Lewis said, "Courage is not simply one of the virtues, but the form of every virtue at the testing point."

But what does "Courage" mean? Nelson Mandela defined it best: "I learned that courage was not the absence of fear, but the triumph over it. The brave man is not he who does not feel afraid, but he who conquers that fear."

In other words, **Courage is not an emotion (like Fear) but a practice—an act of will.** Courage is what we show when we're scared about taking action, but do it anyway.

As with strength training, the more we practice Courage in the face of Fear, the stronger (and bolder) we'll become. And we build up our resilience to handle even more significant challenges as they come.

Courage = Conviction

Before we go further, let's dispel some misconceptions about Courage. It's *not*:

- A lack of fear

- Blind faith

- Recklessness

- Bluster

- Excessive risk-taking

- Vengeance

- Picking a fight.

No. Courage is about being clear-eyed about the dangers that lie ahead but acting anyway. It's an unshakeable conviction that if you fail to act now, you will create an even worse outcome than you feared.

Putting Courage into Practice

How can you become less fearful and more decisive, no matter your challenges?

Follow these three steps for putting Courage into daily practice:

1. Discern the difference between healthy and unhealthy fear.

Not all fear is bad. As entrepreneurs, we can all get too optimistic or even delusional. "This will be a piece of cake. We've got this! No problem." And then you get blindsided.

Healthy fear keeps you and your team in check. You think, "Wait a second. Let's do a reality check here. Does the data support what we're thinking here? Is this something we can execute?"

Healthy fear signals you to pause and evaluate before

finalizing a high-impact decision. "Are we doing the right thing? Do we need to make any other adjustments before moving forward?"

But you have issues when healthy fear crosses the line beyond the "reality check" to become Fear, the vice, which leads to paranoia that impairs your ability to make sound decisions.

2. Adopt the Stockdale Paradox.

In Good to Great: Why Some Companies Make the Leap and Others Don't, Jim Collins introduced the "Stockdale Paradox." It's named after Admiral James Stockdale, the highest-ranking U.S. military officer taken prisoner during the Vietnam War. He endured brutal torture at the "Hanoi Hilton" for eight years, from 1965 to 1973.

During an interview with Stockdale, Collins asked, "Who didn't make it out [of the 'Hanoi Hilton']?"

Stockdale's response surprised Collins: "The optimists. Oh, they were the ones who said, 'We're going to be out by Christmas.' And Christmas would come, and Christmas would go. Then they'd say, 'We're going to be out by Easter.' And Easter would come, and Easter would go. And then Thanksgiving, and then it would be Christmas again. And they died of a broken heart."

Collins continues, "Another long pause and more walking. Then [Stockdale] turned to me and said, 'This is a very important lesson. You must never confuse faith that you will prevail in the end—which you can never afford to lose—with the discipline to confront the most brutal facts of your current reality, whatever they might be.'"

The lesson: When you face situations that cause Fear, don't try to sweep that feeling under the rug of optimism. You'll feel discouraged and lose faith. Instead, apply the Stockdale Paradox. Confront the "brutal facts" of the situation—no matter how bad they seem. And, with Courage, take immediate and ongoing action to improve your situation.

3. Act now.

In *The Greatest Salesman in the World*, Og Mandino writes:

> *My procrastination which has held me back was born of fear and now I recognize this secret mined from the depths of all courageous hearts. Now I know that to conquer fear, I must always act without hesitation, and the flutters in my heart will vanish. Now I know that action reduces the lion of terror to an ant of equanimity. I will act now.*

But how do you make Mandino's "I will act now" mantra a reality in your life? He offers this strategy:

> *I will act now. I will act now. I will act now. Henceforth, I will repeat these words again and again and again, each hour, each day, every day, until the words become as much a habit as my breathing and the actions which follow become as instinctive as the blinking of my eyelids. With these words, I can condition my mind to perform every act necessary for my success. With these words, I can condition my mind to meet every challenge which the failure avoids. I will act now.*

If you learn nothing else from this chapter, take Mandino's mantra to heart. It will transform your life because it trains your mind to push past hesitation to achieve your biggest goals.

Courage at Scale: Courageous Vision

How do you instill the practice of Courage throughout your company?

Follow Churchill's example.

His "Finest Hour" speech offers a powerful framework for helping you set a Courageous Vision and take bold action to get through any challenge that threatens your company's growth.

You can break down the speech into five steps. *(To read the full speech transcript, go to* https://winstonchurchill.org/resources/speeches/1940-the-finest-hour/their-finest-hour/.*)*

Step 1: Set a Courageous Vision.

Define success and communicate your unwavering commitment to achieving it.

> *The disastrous military events which have happened during the past fortnight have not come to me with any sense of surprise. Indeed, I indicated a fortnight ago as clearly as I could to the House that the worst possibilities were open; and I made it perfectly clear then* **that whatever happened in France would make no difference to the resolve of Britain and the British Empire to fight on, if necessary for years, if necessary alone.**

COLLABORATION EFFECT ON PROFIT

To paraphrase Churchill's Courageous Vision: "We will get through this. No matter what. No matter how long. Even with the odds stacked against us."

Step 2: Provide evidence that supports your conviction.

A Courageous Vision not grounded in reality is a delusion. You can't rally people around wishful thinking. So, provide evidence that supports your conviction.

> **We have, therefore, in this Island today a very large and powerful military force.** *This force comprises all our best-trained and our finest troops, including scores of thousands of those who have already measured their quality against the Germans and found themselves at no disadvantage.*

This paragraph is only a sampling of Churchill's evidence. He continues identifying and unpacking several more factors Britain has in its favor.

Do the same thing in your situation. Talk about the reasons why your company *will* succeed despite the obstacles.

Step 3: Confront the (brutal) facts.

As leaders, we often fear speaking with honesty because we don't want the team to "freak out."

Sure, you need discretion in what or how much you share. But don't sugar-coat things. The reality is that your team already knows something is wrong. It's the elephant in the room. They need you to be honest with them, even if it's not the message they want to hear.

Yes. That's easier said than done. But look how Churchill handled it.

> *What General Weygand called the Battle of France is over. I expect that the Battle of Britain is about to begin. Upon this battle depends the survival of Christian civilization. Upon it depends our own British life, and the long continuity of our institutions and our Empire.* **The whole fury and might of the enemy must very soon be turned on us.**

He didn't downplay the situation. Nor did he try to project a fake attitude of strength and bluster. He was candid. He said that despite Britain's strength, it was still vulnerable to the grave threat posed by the Nazis.

Step 4: Count the cost of inaction.

Churchill laid out the stakes, saying (paraphrased), "We have too much at stake to *not* stand up to the Nazis."

> *Hitler knows that he will have to break us in this Island or lose the war. If we can stand up to him, all Europe may be free, and the life of the world may move forward into broad, sunlit uplands.* **But if we fail, then the whole world, including the United States, including all that we have known and cared for, will sink into the abyss of a new Dark Age made more sinister, and perhaps more protracted, by the lights of perverted science.**

The lesson: If you want to get yourself and your team over the fear of taking bold action, consider the stakes. You'll lose more if you *don't* act.

Step 5: Paint a vivid picture of success.

As Churchill closed his speech, he described what Britain's legacy would look like if they prevailed.

> *Let us, therefore, brace ourselves to our duties, and so bear ourselves that,* **if the British Empire and its Commonwealth last for a thousand years, men will still say, 'This was their finest hour.'**

When gripped by Fear, we tend to obsess with the worst-case scenario. We think, "If I fire this abusive client, we'll lose all that business and have to let good people go."

Perhaps. But what about the potential upside of making the hard decision? What would that look like?

Your employees would see a strong leader who has their back—someone they can believe in and willingly follow no matter the dangers that lie ahead.

Now, you have a more enthusiastic team that works hard to replace the lost revenue and put the company on a faster growth trajectory.

And that tough decision could prove to be your company's "finest hour."

The Bottom Line

Maya Angelou put it best: "I am convinced that courage is the most important of all the virtues. Because without courage, you cannot practice any other virtue consistently."

Without Courage, how can you practice Humility, Empathy, Acceptance, or any of the Great 8 Virtues? You can't. Courage is necessary for taking action that makes a virtuous life and business possible.

In the Trenches: Feeling the Fear But Doing It Anyway

David Harper

You know deep down in your heart what you need to do. It's time to do it. But you're experiencing a crisis of belief.

That's the vice of Fear sowing the seeds of doubt in your mind and clouding your judgment.

The following are the internal Fear-based conversations in the minds of founders and non-founder leaders in the hundreds of companies we've consulted with over the last 25 years.

Founders:

- You need to let your VP of sales go. He's toxic to the leadership team. But you keep telling yourself, "There's too much at stake with the company. What if…[insert the worst-case scenarios that come to mind]?"

- You know you need to delegate more to your leadership team and get out of the "center of the circle," but you're waffling: "What if they drop the ball? Then what?"

- You know you want to announce a dramatic change in moving the business forward, but you think, "What if they don't buy it?"

- You know you should include your leadership team in your long-term transition plan—you're convinced that selling the company to a third party is the best option—but you think, "What if they don't like the idea and leave?"

- You know that to accomplish everything needed, you must be aggressive in the long-range forecasts, but you tend to "sandbag"—saying I am just conservative by nature! I don't want to set a too ambitious goal we may be unable to hit."

Non-Founder Leaders:

- You should address the issue, but no one is saying anything. "Does anyone else notice how this is wrong and hurting our company? It's the elephant in the room, but he's the CEO. I could get fired if I speak up!"

- You have a great idea that could make the company better and more profitable if you were free to execute it. But you feel your hands are tied. You also find yourself constantly waiting for permission. And on the rare occasion you step out to say something, you often get shut down. "I need to state my case, but what if .....?"

- You sense things are off track. And if you keep going in the same direction, it won't end well. But you hesitate to say anything as thoughts like these hold you back:

  - "We need a new way forward, but I wonder what would happen if I brought it up."

  - "I wonder what Bill's plans are for the company, but he isn't saying anything. I guess I should just keep my mouth shut."

  - "I can do more than this, but I'm not putting myself out there. I might look bad!"

Fear is debilitating. It keeps you from saying what needs to be said. It causes everyone to lose.

The path forward is practicing the virtue of Courage. It enables you to cast an exciting vision of what *could be*. And it gives you the faith and strength to pursue that vision against all odds and obstacles.

> What we've seen in others—and have experienced in ourselves—is that once you get a taste of that preferred future, that clearly stated vision, you can't ever go back to the status quo.

Deeper Reflection

1. What's an example of a situation where you misinterpreted Fear as wisdom?

2. From your perspective, where is the line between wisdom and Fear?

3. To what extent has Fear undermined your leadership effectiveness?

4. What's at stake? What's the cost to you and your company if you don't keep the vice of Fear in check?

5. Who can you point to as an excellent role model for practicing Courage? What traits do you see in them that demonstrate their Courage?

6. How would you rate your Courage on a scale of 1 to 10, with 10 being the highest? What would you need to change to move your rating from your current number to a 10?

7. What's your Courageous Vision for your company?

8. Why believe you and your team can live up to that Vision? In other words, what's the evidence that supports your conviction?

9. What potential obstacles could hold the company back? How can you and your team confront and mitigate those risks preemptively?

10. Imagine you and your team practicing Courage at a high level. What would that look like? How would you describe the difference in your company? What would be the impact on your bottom line?

Remember:

You will confront situations where Fear grips you—that's a given. But Courage is the decision to move forward anyway, refusing to allow the uncertainty ahead to overwhelm your resolve to succeed.

PART 3:
ALIGN INTERESTS—AND INCENTIVES—WITH THE 3 WINS FRAMEWORK

CHAPTER 11:
INCENTIVIZING THE VIRTUES
(NOT THE VICES)

"Culture isn't just one aspect of the game; it is the game. In the end, an organization is nothing more than the collective capacity of its people to create value."

- Lou Gerstner

A few years ago, we received valuable feedback from a long-time client regarding our email newsletter on The Great 8 Virtues.

This exchange sparked an epiphany for our company and played a pivotal role in inspiring us to write this book.

"I appreciate your articles, and we've started implementing many of the concepts," he said. "But I'm curious. Legacy Advisory Partners is a financial services company. What does cultivating a virtuous culture have to do with financial services?"

Well...*Everything.*

That's because smart financial strategies—such as long-term incentive plans, company-owned life insurance (COLI), and non-qualified deferred compensation plans—yield the best outcomes in companies that nurture a high-trust, virtuous culture.

Without the Great 8 Virtues as your guide, even the most well-intentioned performance incentives may inadvertently encourage negative behaviors—such as Greed, Territorialism, and Egotism—that could jeopardize your business.

Misaligned Incentives: The Enron Collapse

Take Enron, for example.

The once seventh-largest company in the United States collapsed in 2001 because of widespread fraud and corruption despite operating under four publicly stated core values—Respect, Integrity, Communication, and Excellence.

Behind closed doors, the company's aggressive push for growth at all costs created a culture of deception. Employees, driven by the allure of bonuses and stock options, found themselves entangled in a web of lies, falsifying financial reports to paint a rosy picture of the company's health.

How did this dysfunction occur?

Enron rewarded the wrong behaviors. Let's break down how Enron's misaligned incentives undermined each core value, leading to unintended consequences that sunk the company.

Value #1: Respect

The company professed to treat its employees, customers, and partners with respect, emphasizing diversity and the importance of treating everyone fairly.

Misalignment: Enron introduced a performance review system called the Performance Review Committee (PRC), which aimed to identify and reward top performers, intending to promote a meritocracy within the company. But the PRC was also known as the "rank and yank" or "forced ranking" system. Employees were ranked against one another, and those in the bottom 10-20% were fired or pressured to leave.

The PRC process became highly competitive and cutthroat, fostering an environment where employees sabotaged, backstabbed, and undermined their colleagues to secure higher rankings. Instead of promoting respect, it created a toxic culture of mistrust and fear.

The Vice(s) at Work: Territorialism

Value #2: Integrity

The company touted strong ethical principles like honesty, transparency, and accountability.

Misalignment: Enron established a bonus structure tied to the company's stock price and earnings, intending to align the interests of executives and employees with the company's financial success. But executives focused on meeting short-term financial targets to inflate their bonuses. This behavior led to executives gaming the system by manipulating the company's financial reports.

For example:

- Enron used special purpose entities (SPEs) to hide debt and losses, creating the illusion of a financially healthy company.

- Enron's management manipulated earnings by booking future expected profits as current revenue, deceiving investors and stakeholders about the company's financial performance.

- Executives provided false information to regulators and auditors, breaching their ethical obligations.

The Vice(s) at Work: Greed, Dishonesty

Value #3: Communication

Enron claimed to value open and honest communication to encourage teamwork and collaboration across all levels of the organization.

Misalignment: Enron's "rank and yank" performance review system stifled open communication. It discouraged employees from bringing up potential problems or concerns because they feared the repercussions of admitting failure or raising issues—and losing their jobs.

The Vice(s) at Work: Dishonesty, Fear

Value #4: Excellence

The company aimed for outstanding performance, innovation, and continuous improvement.

Misalignment: Enron offered significant financial rewards for employees who hit their targets and contributed to the company's growth. But instead of focusing on delivering outstanding performance, key executives were preoccupied with manipulating financial statements to project an image of success. The company's obsession with increasing its stock price and pleasing Wall Street overshadowed the need for operational excellence, innovation, and continuous improvement for long-term, sustainable success.

The Vice(s) at Work: Egotism, Greed, Dishonesty

Enron's collapse teaches us, as owners, that we must be intentional about aligning our financial incentives with the Great 8 Virtues, not the vices. Otherwise, we'll unwittingly reward behaviors that poison the culture and kill the business.

Red Flags to Look For

How do you design an incentive strategy that promotes the virtues and not the vices in your company?

The first step is to uncover any issues with your current incentives by looking for red flags like these:

Poor teamwork.

Root cause: Incentives are tied more to individual than team performance. This creates an environment where employees work in silos, limiting knowledge sharing and collaboration that could benefit the company as a whole.

Disengaged employees.

Root cause: Incentives are based on unclear or poorly defined criteria. This causes employees to feel confused or demotivated by the lack of transparency, reducing their engagement and productivity.

Increased quality issues.

Root cause: Incentives are based on aggressive production quotas. This leads to increased errors and decreased quality as employees take shortcuts to meet deadlines, jeopardizing the company's reputation and long-term growth.

Excessive customer complaints and churn.

Root cause: Incentives based on overly ambitious cost-cutting measures. This rewards employees for cutting corners to boost short-term profits. But customers get angry about receiving less value for their money and decide to leave for a competitor.

Tunnel vision.

Root cause: Incentives are tied to narrow performance measures. This causes employees to focus solely on hitting those targets, neglecting other essential aspects of their jobs.

Hoarding resources.

Root cause: Bonuses are tied to departmental budget savings. This leads to managers hoarding resources or underinvesting in necessary tools and training to save budget at the expense of company growth.

These are only a few examples of red flags. The key is to look at what's not working in your business because chances are strong that a misaligned incentive is at the root of the problem.

The 3 Wins: Aligning Interests, Incentives, and the Virtues

Now, let's return to our client's question at the start of this chapter: "What does cultivating a virtuous culture have to do with financial services?"

And we said, "Everything." That's because **we believe a virtuous culture is like healthy soil where the "seeds" (your financial strategies) can truly take hold, grow, and multiply.** Otherwise, you will struggle to keep an increasingly dysfunctional company afloat.

But the more we pondered that question, the more we realized we needed to be explicit about "connecting the dots" for our clients.

But how? How could we help them achieve proper alignment between their company's incentives, their (and their team's) interests, and the Great 8 Virtues?

That's when we began to form the idea of The 3 Wins—a framework that would tie everything together. And we'll start unpacking The 3 Wins Framework for you in the next chapter.

CHAPTER 12:
ONE FRAMEWORK. THREE WINS. FULL ALIGNMENT.

◆—————————•—————————◆

> *If everyone is moving forward together,*
> *then success takes care of itself.*
> **- Henry Ford**

What began as a typical financial services engagement in 2018 would ultimately lead to our discovery of a new decision-making framework that has since transformed our business. And it has produced breakthrough results for our clients who have adopted it.

That framework is what we now call "The 3 Wins."

The Need for a Wider-View Lens

At that time, we met with five shareholder partners of a management consulting firm about a non-qualified long-term incentive plan (LTIP) to retain their key leaders.

An LTIP is a compensation plan that provides financial rewards to executives based on performance metrics or goals over an extended period and is not subject to specific regulatory requirements like qualified plans, such as a 401k. Now, when you design one of these plans, you want to customize it to fit your company by addressing questions such as:

- Who will be included as the plan's participants? In other words, who do I want to incentivize and retain?

- What company benchmarks do the participants need to pursue to earn the award?

- What plan design features best fit the shareholders, company, and participants (e.g., vesting schedule, distributions, funding)?

- How do we communicate the plan and the benchmarks so that participants see the opportunity for their long-term success with the company?

But we hit a roadblock when all five shareholders couldn't get on the same page with their answers. The problem: The partners didn't have clear, agreed-upon objectives and benchmarks for the company to help guide their decisions in designing a successful LTIP.

They first needed a shared vision around the company's purpose, direction, vision, and goals. **Without this alignment, the shareholders risked incentivizing their key leaders to pursue "good" goals at the expense of the company's "best" goals that inspire the highest level of collaboration and performance.**

COLLABORATION EFFECT ON PROFIT

"Good" goals appear to be worthy targets but have hidden downsides. For example:

- **Fast growth:** Rapidly entering new markets can boost sales but may strain your ability to serve those new customers effectively, jeopardizing your company's reputation.

- **Cost cutting:** Slashing costs may increase short-term profit but risk long-term growth by compromising product quality or cutting corners in service.

- **Individual performance rewards:** Individual performance bonuses can boost specific results but may hinder overall company collaboration and success.

But the "best" goals serve the interests of all stakeholders—the company, its owners, and its key leaders. For example:

- **Sustainable growth:** Prioritizing steady and sustainable growth over quick wins ensures the company can maintain its success in the long run.

- **Quality assurance:** Prioritizing product or service quality improves customer satisfaction and bolsters your company's reputation.

- **Team collaboration incentives**: Creating reward goals based on team achievements builds a culture of collaboration, ensuring all members are working towards the same objectives.

If the shareholders couldn't agree on the best goals for the company, their LTIP would likely breed resentment towards the key leaders participating in the plan.

That's because, in these situations, we often see the vices of Fear, Greed, and Territorialism begin to creep in:

- *How can we afford to award that much money to the participants?*

- *Are we paying out too much to people who aren't shareholders?*

In the end, the shareholders might be tempted to cut the plan short instead of staying the course guided by well-thought-out, predefined benchmarks.

We realized that if an LTIP was going to help them succeed, they needed to take a step back and look at their plan—and its potential impact on their business—through a wider-view "3 Wins" lens.

A Holistic Approach to Financial Decision-Making

The 3 Wins is a framework we've developed at Legacy Advisory Partners that takes a holistic and balanced approach to financial decision-making.

The idea is to design incentive strategies that create full alignment—where all three parties "win" simultaneously:

- The shareholder(s)
- The company
- The key-leaders.

Otherwise, if one party wins, but one or two of the others do not, *everyone* ultimately loses.

So, if you want an incentive strategy to succeed for the long haul, you must set it up so that all stakeholders win.

And that's what we helped our client achieve by applying these three steps of The 3 Wins Framework to their LTIP decisions:

Step 1: Begin with the Shareholder Win.

How does the incentive plan improve the shareholder's path to leaving a financial legacy to their family?

The Shareholder Win is about securing your financial legacy.

After all, as an owner, you didn't take on the risk and invest your blood, sweat, and tears in the business just to earn a paycheck. You're building an opportunity to establish a financial legacy for your family—starting with financial independence. The company is an asset you expect will provide you with sufficient annual profits and market value to support the lifestyle you'd like to live when you're ready to exit your company or otherwise move out of the day-to-day as an owner-operator.

So, you should consider taking owner distributions to diversify your retirement assets beyond the company's potential market valuation. Otherwise, you could be jeopardizing your financial future.

And that was the challenge for our client. Although the shareholders had good salaries, they weren't taking owner distributions from the company's earnings.

Why?

They didn't have clarity on the company's cash-flow requirements—a critical piece to the Company Win. So, their default mode was to keep the cash in the business because "we don't know what will happen in the future."

"You need some kind of endpoint," we advised. "Does it make sense to keep piling up cash in the business? You've got to collectively decide how much is enough reserve for the company to feel good about the future. And anything above that, put that money to work in the right ways that serve your goals."

We showed them how taking consistent distributions would help them:

- Foster better long-term thinking and decision-making

- Make the Shareholder Win more tangible because they would be able to taste some of the fruit of the company's earnings

- Reduce the risk of resentment when paying out awards to key leaders because they would also feel the "win."

And distributions would give them more staying power because the shareholders could loan money back to the company if the company goes through a downturn.

So, we walked them through the process of building a growth model that gave them better visibility into their cash flow needs, net income, budgets, retained earnings and reinvestment targets, and distribution opportunities for lifestyle and other investments.

Once the partners agreed to take consistent owner distributions, they began to find alignment in defining their Shareholder Win, individually and collectively.

And that gave them greater clarity on how to set the LTIP benchmarks for the key leaders in a way that protected the Shareholder Win, too.

Step 2: Define the Company Win.

> *How does the incentive plan improve the company's short- and long-term growth and marketability prospects?*

The Company Win is about caring for the goose that lays the golden eggs.

If the company doesn't have a courageous vision based on sound numbers and talented people, it will struggle to succeed. And if the company can't win, neither can the shareholders nor the key leaders. The 3 Wins must remain in balance.

So, we worked with the client to set clear and realistic long-term targets for their business. We then helped them determine how the shareholders and key leaders can best collaborate to achieve those targets.

> *"If we create enough of an advantage to achieve our Shareholder Win and the Company Win, we will award $X to the incentive plan for our key leaders to participate in the success they helped create."*

But how do you choose a good benchmark that aligns The 3 Wins?

Make it a profitability target—a stretch goal beyond the company's typical performance. For example, suppose your company's baseline is $10 million in revenue at 10% ($1 million) gross profit. Let's say you and your team set a stretch goal of $12 million in revenue at 13% ($1.56 million) gross profit.

So, if the shareholders, key leaders, and other stakeholders collaborate and achieve this goal, the company would generate an extra $560,000 in profit.

You would then pay the incentive award *only* when the company wins by earning profit beyond the $1 million baseline.

If the company hits the stretch goal, you would pay out the long-term incentive award from the $560,000 in extra earnings.

You would then decide how to allocate the $560,000 based on how you've defined The 3 Wins. Your allocation might look something like this:

- $300,000 to the LTIP
- $100,000 back into the company
- $160,000 to additional shareholder distributions.

The critical point here is that whatever benchmarks and payout allocations you decide, make sure your company gets what it needs to keep "laying the golden eggs."

Step 3: Ensure the Key-Leader Win

> *How does the incentive improve the key leader's path to their own financial legacy and career fulfillment?*

And this leads us to the Key Leader Win. Your key leaders are those executives essential to your company's success and the most difficult to replace.

The idea here is that when you help your leaders achieve their personal financial goals, they will have a stronger incentive to collaborate, contributing to the Company Win—and, ultimately, your Shareholder Win.

Our original conversation with the management consulting firm started with the Key-Leader Win—an opportunity for their executives to participate in the success they help create for the company.

But we couldn't help them choose the plan's particulars until they first defined their Shareholder and Company wins.

Now, they had the clarity to:

- Decide who will participate in the plan
- Set the company target—a stretch goal—for earning the award
- Tailor the plan to fit their objectives and keep The 3 Wins in balance
- Communicate effectively with the plan's participants to get their buy-in and commitment to collaborate at the highest level.

To ensure the Key-Leader Win aligns with the Shareholder and Company wins, they based the incentive awards on achieving a collective and collaborative goal, not individual or departmental performance.

Full Alignment = The Collaboration Effect on Profit

The 3 Wins has since become our standard operating procedure for creating alignment within our company. And it's helping our clients do the same. We encourage you to adopt it as your financial decision-making model, too.

That's because when you achieve complete alignment with The 3 Wins, you get to witness everyone on your team rowing in the same direction.

When you combine The 3 Wins with The Great 8 Virtues discussed in Chapters 3-10, you will build a high-trust, high-performance culture that attracts the most talented people to rally around your vision. You'll see senior leaders and rank-and-file employees all working together in their optimal roles toward the same goal, reaching a level of collaboration that becomes a force multiplier to achieve breakthrough results for your company.

That's precisely what the Collaboration Effect on Profit looks like in action: When you align incentives and interests in a way that gets everyone "rowing in the same direction," the shareholders win, the company wins, and the key leaders win.

In short, *all stakeholders* win.

Over the next three chapters, we'll dive deeper into each Win with practical strategies and tips to help you achieve the full alignment that will unleash the Collaboration Effect on Profit in your business.

Ready to grow?

Let's go!

CHAPTER 13:
THE SHAREHOLDER WIN: LAYING THE FOUNDATION FOR YOUR FINANCIAL LEGACY

> *"The great danger for most of us lies not in setting our aim too high and falling short; but in setting our aim too low, and achieving our mark."*
> ## - Michelangelo

T he president of a construction firm referred a subcontractor to us to see if The 3 Wins Framework could help them.

"Their quality of work is exceptional," he said. "But we're starting to get concerned they won't have the capacity to keep up with our growth."

The subcontractor is led by Josh (not his real name), the founder of a 20-person mechanical contracting company. On the surface, the firm had all the markings of success. He hired skilled technicians, landed substantial contracts, and built a stable of loyal clients to grow the company to $7 million in annual revenue.

But a closer look revealed that the company's growth had hit a ceiling with Josh as the sole executive, who wore too many hats in the business.

Stuck in the Center of the Circle

When we first met with Josh, he was "leading from the center of the circle"—where all critical decision-making ran through him. (See Chapter 3: "Humility vs. Egotism" to dig deeper into how to break out of the center of the circle.)

He exhibited a classic symptom of Founder's Syndrome: "If I want things done the right way, I'll do it myself."

Josh acknowledged he had become the bottleneck. He also came to understand the importance of building a leadership team to help him scale the business. But he couldn't see how the company could afford it.

Yet, if things didn't change—and quickly—Josh risked losing one of his biggest clients.

Typically, when we encounter situations like Josh's, we find it's because the founder hasn't defined their Shareholder Win.

As a result, they're trapped in a survival-stage mentality. The vice of Busyness grabs hold, causing them to feel so overwhelmed with putting out day-to-day fires that they have zero margin for thinking strategically about their business. (See Chapter 4: "Empathy vs. Busyness.")

And that's where Josh was.

But something clicked as we worked with him to define his Shareholder Win.

For the first time, he could see the possibilities—the lifestyle and legacy he could create for his family.

But if he was going to have a realistic shot at achieving his ambitious financial goals, he could no longer afford to be the sole executive of a business stuck in survival mode. He needed to build the company beyond survival with a strong leadership team to help him "win."

And that simple mindset shift—from survival to abundance—has put Josh on a trajectory to hit his targets in the next 15 years.

The Shareholder Win Defined

What is the Shareholder Win?

The Shareholder Win is about getting beyond "survival mode" to build a sustainably profitable business that produces the means you need to build an impactful financial legacy in your family for generations to come.

Financial legacy refers to the financial assets, philanthropic and charitable values, and planning and strategies you leave behind for your heirs or beneficiaries. It encompasses not only material wealth like money, property, and investments but also intangibles like financial (and often spiritual) philosophies, values, and habits that you would like to impart to the next generations.

There are five parts to the Shareholder Win:

- Financial independence
- Ownership transition planning
- Estate and tax planning
- Family legacy planning
- Wealth management.

Think of each part as a building block, one stacked upon the other, to help you create, protect, and perpetuate the lifestyle and legacy you dream about.

So, how do you define *your* Shareholder Win?

Part 1: Financial Independence

Begin by setting your financial independence target.

What's your number? How much do you need—apart from your company's value—to sustain your desired lifestyle indefinitely without additional employment income? (We refer to this as being financially independent *from* your company.) What's your timeline for reaching that number? What's your plan to get there?

Consider Jane:

Jane owns a successful software-as-a-service (SaaS) company she started 10 years ago. Her company has grown steadily and now has a team of 50 people, with annual revenues of $18 million and net profits of $4 million.

Suppose her financial independence "number" to sustain her lifestyle and charitable giving goals is $20 million. How does Jane put herself in the best position to hit her mark? Here are the factors she would likely consider:

Building a Team of Experts: Jane assembles a team of financial advisors, tax professionals, and other experts to develop and validate her financial independence plan. They also provide ongoing, periodic advice to help her adjust the plan when necessary to keep her on track.

The Company Win: With her "number" in mind, Jane sets an ambitious yet realistic growth target for the business that aligns with her financial independence goals. (We'll break down the Company Win in the next chapter.)

The Key-Leader Win: Jane empowers her leaders to "win" by allowing them to participate in the company's success that they helped create, aligning their interests and incentives with her goals. (We'll dig deeper into the Key-Leader Win in Chapter 15.)

Owner Distributions: Jane takes owner distributions when the company hits specific benchmarks. This way, she can reduce her risk by placing that additional income into other assets outside her business.

Personal Savings & Investments: Jane has diversified her financial portfolio. Apart from reinvesting in her business, she has robust personal savings, retirement accounts, and other investments like real estate and stocks. She is no longer solely dependent on her company for income.

Emergency Fund: She and her business have a cushion of savings to survive any unplanned disruptions for an extended period without requiring her to sell assets, go into debt, or place unnecessary pressure and stress on her company and team.

The Most Profitable Exit Strategy: Jane has options. Thanks to her diversified investments, she doesn't have to be in a hurry to sell the business. She can wait until she gets the best deal. Alternatively, she could hire a capable CEO to run the company while she takes on a more passive or strategic role.

Charitable Giving: Now that she's financially secure, Jane can continue contributing meaningfully to causes she cares about. She establishes a charitable foundation with an endowment that provides grants to projects focused on education and healthcare.

By integrating charitable giving, Jane's definition of financial independence becomes more holistic. It allows her to extend the benefits of her financial freedom to others, creating a lasting impact beyond her immediate personal or business circle for generations to come.

Part 2: Ownership Transition Planning

The next building block for the Shareholder Win is ownership transition planning. The goal is to create a blueprint for transferring the business to achieve your financial independence objectives while setting the stage for continued success under new ownership.

How do you plan for a smooth transition?

Consider John:

John has been running a successful manufacturing company for 25 years. Five years ago, he began considering retirement and started his transition planning process.

His process might look something like this:

Early Planning: John starts by identifying his objectives and time frame for retirement, aiming for a transition five years later.

Consulting Experts: He assembles a team of advisors, including a financial advisor, a business valuation expert, and a business transition attorney, to guide him through the process.

Valuation and Financial Assessment: A thorough business valuation is conducted. His team also assesses the tax implications of various transition options.

Succession Planning: After evaluating his internal team and family members, John decides his best option is to sell to an external buyer. He trains his management team to ensure the business can operate without him, making it more attractive to buyers.

Business Optimization: He spends the next few years streamlining operations, cutting costs where possible, and building a solid client base to maximize the business valuation.

Legal Preparations: All business agreements, contracts, and potential legal hurdles are reviewed and put in order.

Market Readiness: His team prepares a detailed information packet for potential buyers, highlighting the business's strengths, opportunities, and valuation metrics.

Stakeholder Communication: John communicates his plans transparently with key staff and stakeholders at an appropriate time, helping to manage expectations and reduce uncertainty.

Due Diligence and Sale: Once a credible buyer is identified, John's team efficiently manages the due diligence process. Negotiations go smoothly because both parties have clear expectations and all necessary information.

In this scenario, John adds to his Shareholder Win by getting the amount he wants from his company when he leaves. But, throughout the process, he also has to balance the Company Win (to maximize the valuation) and the Key-Leader Win (by communicating transparently and ensuring the leadership team is incentivized to stay on board).

Part 3: Estate and Tax Planning

When you've worked hard to achieve your financial independence goals, how do you prepare to pass on that "win" to the people and causes you care about the most?

How do you ensure a smooth transfer of ownership and control of *all* your assets upon retirement, incapacity, or death?

The estate planning process aims to maximize the value of your estate by reducing taxes and other expenses while also providing financial security to heirs and ensuring the business continues to operate successfully. It may involve a variety of legal instruments and strategies, including wills, trusts, buy-sell agreements, succession plans, and tax optimization methods.

Whatever you do, don't put off your estate planning because you think you have plenty of time or believe you don't have enough assets to worry about passing on. Start planning as soon as possible, no matter how far away you are from reaching your financial independence goals.

Consider Sarah:

Sarah has built her catering business from the ground up and turned it into a local success story. She's deeply involved in every aspect of the company and keeps most of the operational knowledge in her head. She hasn't drafted a formal estate plan because she's too busy running the business and believes she has plenty of time to plan later.

Then Sarah unexpectedly passes away with a sudden illness, leaving behind her husband, Mark, and two adult children, Emily and Josh.

What Does the Aftermath Look Like for the Business?

Lack of Succession Planning: The sudden loss of Sarah leads to immediate operational challenges. No one else in the business has the full breadth of her knowledge or client relationships. Employees become anxious about job security, and key clients look elsewhere.

Legal Complications: Because Sarah died without a will, her assets, including the business, must go through probate. The court appoints Mark as the administrator, but he has little experience with the business and struggles to keep it afloat.

Tax Consequences: The business has to be assessed for estate tax purposes, and because Sarah never engaged in tax planning, a significant chunk of the business value is owed in taxes. Mark has to sell off some of the business assets to cover the tax bill.

Protecting the Family Interest: Shares of the business flow into Mark's estate. Mark then marries Jennifer. When Mark passes away, the value of the business goes to Jennifer—not Sarah's intended heirs and beneficiaries.

What's the Impact On the Family?

Financial Insecurity: Sarah's family depended on the business's income. So, with the company struggling and assets being sold to pay taxes, the family faces financial hardship.

Family Discord: Emily wants to take over the business, but Josh is more interested in selling it and splitting the proceeds. The absence of a clear succession plan or directives from Sarah leads to arguments and tension among family members.

Unexpected Debts: The family is exposed to business debts and liabilities they never anticipated, further straining their finances.

Don't be Sarah. Protect your Shareholder Win by developing an estate plan as soon as possible to ensure your family—and business—won't lose if the "unexpected" ever happens to you.

Part 4: Family Legacy Planning

The family legacy plan is the pinnacle of the Shareholder Win. It ensures you can share your "win" with the people and causes you to care about the most for future generations, according to your values and pre-set terms. This way, you'll always have a say in how your wealth gets managed and distributed long after you're gone.

The idea here is you can't manage your finances from the grave, but you can establish guidelines and instill

values in the next generation of leaders and decision-makers in your family.

What's involved with family legacy planning?

Consider Elizabeth:

Elizabeth owns a real estate development company valued at around $100 million. She has four children—Maggie, Jack, Emily, and Sam. Maggie is an architect involved in the family business. Jack is a lawyer, Emily is an artist, and Sam is in college studying environmental science. Elizabeth has always been a supporter of the arts and environmental conservation.

Elizabeth's family legacy planning process might look something like this:

Long-Term Vision: Elizabeth initiates legacy planning discussions as soon as her business achieves substantial growth. She is clear about her goals: to sustain the business, support the arts and environment, and maintain family unity.

Family Collaboration: Elizabeth invites a consultant to lead a series of family meetings, including her spouse and children, to outline her vision, request their input, and gain their buy-in.

Role Identification: Roles and responsibilities are clearly defined. Maggie would take over the business. Jack would handle legal matters for both the company and the family foundation. Emily would be responsible for the arts sector of the foundation, and Sam for the environmental side.

Legal Structures: Elizabeth consults with professionals to set up trusts, wills, and a family foundation with clear objectives related to arts and environmental support.

Business Succession: A detailed succession plan is developed for Maggie to take over, including mentorship phases, and a board of advisors is set up for added governance.

Philanthropic Vehicle: Elizabeth establishes the family foundation with endowments and clear directives on the percentage of business profits to be contributed annually.

Financial Education: Elizabeth invests in financial literacy programs for the entire family, including the grandchildren, to ensure everyone understands wealth management.

Transparency: All plans are well-documented and shared with family members, ensuring total transparency.

Tax Planning: Efficient tax planning is incorporated into the wealth transfer plans to ensure minimal taxation and maximum resource allocation for the family and charitable initiatives.

Inter-Generational Engagement: Grandchildren become increasingly involved in the family business and foundation, ensuring the legacy continues.

In this scenario, Elizabeth gains the peace of mind of knowing her life's work will continue in alignment with her vision of family unity, business growth, and social contributions for future generations.

Part 5: Wealth Management

The previous four parts of the Shareholder Win pertain to setting your targets and creating realistic plans for achieving them.

But how do you successfully execute those plans? How do you stay on track as market dynamics and risk tolerances fluctuate over time?

That's where the final building block of the Shareholder Win comes in—wealth management.

Unlike traditional asset management, which primarily focuses on individual assets and financial planning, wealth management for business owners integrates personal and business financial strategies to maximize growth, liquidity, and profitability while minimizing risk and tax liability.

Your approach should be customized to you, considering you have a significant portion of your wealth tied up in your business and face unique challenges such as cyclical cash flows, complex taxation, and succession issues.

What does effective ongoing wealth management look like?

Consider Emily:

Emily owns a successful women's apparel brand. She consults a team of professionals, including a financial advisor, tax consultant, and estate attorney, to help her with objectives such as:

General Planning: Emily has a 5-year and 10-year financial plan, reviewed annually with her financial advisor. Her business and personal financial goals are clearly defined and aligned.

Investment Management: Emily has a diversified investment portfolio. She has wisely separated her investments from her business investments, ensuring her net worth is not overly dependent on her business.

Business Valuation and Succession Planning: She regularly assesses her business valuation and has a succession plan in place. She has also set up a buy-sell agreement with minority partners to ensure business continuity in unexpected situations.

Tax Planning: Her tax consultant helps her optimize personal and business taxes, taking advantage of all possible deductions and credits. She has set up her business structure in a tax-efficient way.

Retirement Planning: Emily contributes the maximum to her personal and employer-sponsored retirement accounts. Her financial independence plans are not solely dependent on selling her business.

Risk Management: Comprehensive insurance policies are in place for her personal life (life, health, disability) and business (liability, property, business interruption).

Estate Planning: Her will and estate plan are updated and reviewed regularly. She has set up trusts to facilitate wealth transfer and minimize estate taxes.

Liquidity Management: Emily maintains a separate emergency fund for her personal life and business. She also has a line of credit for unforeseen business expenses.

Debt Management: Personal or business-related debt is structured to have the lowest interest rates. Emily follows a plan to pay off debts while balancing growth and investment.

Ongoing Review: Emily conducts quarterly reviews of her business and personal finances with her team of professionals.

They adjust plans as needed based on performance metrics and changing life circumstances.

This comprehensive and customized approach to wealth management provides you with financial security and peace of mind, knowing you're on the right track to achieving your Shareholder Win.

Beware of Imbalance

When applying The 3 Wins Framework to your business, the starting point is to define your Shareholder Win. But your win cannot be at the company's or key leaders' expense. Otherwise, everyone loses, including you.

That's why it's critical to protect yourself against the vices like Greed (See Chapter 6: "Accountability vs. Greed") to keep the Shareholder Win in proper balance.

For example, some owners get tempted to withdraw more money from the company than they should to support their increasingly extravagant lifestyle.

They rationalize to themselves, "This is *my* company. I deserve to get what I want when I want it."

So, they buy luxury cars, boats, and multiple high-end properties and take lavish vacations, even when they (and the business) can't really afford it.

That's winning, right?

Sure. In the short term.

However, their business will have less cash to manage daily expenses, hindering its ability to handle unforeseen challenges or take advantage of new opportunities. And the key leaders may choose to leave the company if they perceive the owner's behavior as detrimental to the business or if they feel their hard work isn't being rewarded or reinvested in the company's growth.

How can you counteract the temptation of Greed to keep the Shareholder Win in proper balance? Apply The Great 8 virtue of Accountability by instilling internal controls such as:

- **Transparency and reporting:** Regular and transparent financial reporting can shed light on how funds are used, making it harder for the owner to misuse them.

- **Long-term incentive plans:** When employees have a stake in the company's success, there is an additional layer of oversight and vested interest in financial decisions.

- **External audits:** Regular audits by a third party can keep the owner accountable.

By implementing these measures, you can create a system of checks and balances to ensure your personal financial decisions don't adversely affect the business.

The Bottom Line

Bill Copeland said, "The trouble with not having a goal is that you can spend your life running up and down the field and never score."

Can you relate? Do you ever feel like Josh did at the beginning of this chapter—overwhelmed with "running up and down the field" but unable to find the goal line?

If so, change that today. Begin defining your Shareholder Win so you can start moving the ball across the field—and putting up big points on your scoreboard.

The Next Steps

Here are the immediate steps you can take this week to begin the process of defining your Shareholder Win:

1. Dream.

Schedule an hour this week to journal, brainstorm, and dream about the lifestyle and legacy you want to build for your family. Write it down!

2. Assemble.

Begin assembling a team of advisors—including financial advisors, tax professionals, and other experts—by identifying potential candidates and scheduling meetings to meet and vet them.

3. Set.

Set deadlines for when you want to have addressed each of the five parts of your Shareholder Win.

CHAPTER 14:
THE COMPANY WIN: FEEDING (AND PROTECTING) THE GOLDEN GOOSE

"The balance between the golden egg (production) and the health and welfare of the goose (production capability) is often a difficult judgment call. But I suggest it is the very essence of effectiveness."
- Stephen Covey

We introduced Alex to The 3 Wins Framework when his company was at a crossroads.

As the majority shareholder CEO of an $80 million manufacturing company, Alex was wrestling with a critical decision. Should he fire his company's president, Benjamin, a minority shareholder, or hold off and see if things improve?

Deep down, Alex knew the right move. For over five years, his trusted advisors had spoken in unison that he should cut ties. But now, time was running out. Three key leaders had already left when a fourth handed in her resignation.

What was he going to do?

When the 'Golden Goose' Gets Sick

About 15 years earlier, Alex hired a young marketing talent, Benjamin, fresh out of college. Benjamin was not just any recruit; he was the son of a long-time family friend. Over the years, Alex mentored Benjamin, treating him as a protégé, hoping to instill the values and vision required to guide the company into the future.

Eager to cement Benjamin's commitment to the firm, Alex offered him a 20% equity share when promoting him to president about six years ago. It was a bold gesture to ensure Benjamin's decisions would align with the company's long-term success.

But things didn't pan out as expected. Gradually, Benjamin's behavior started to deviate from the company's ethos. He took his position for granted, and the vices—Greed, Egotism, Territorialism, and Anger—began to emerge in his character and leadership style.

Benjamin's vices became the "viruses" that infected the company—the proverbial "goose that lays the golden eggs." Under Benjamin's tenure as president:

- He used company funds to upgrade his office extravagantly, far surpassing the functional needs of his role. Company cars, accommodations, and even business trips became more about showcasing his status than actual business needs.

- He slashed funding for the Research & Development department, emphasizing immediate sales over developing innovative products. This move juiced the company's short-term earnings but hindered its long-term growth by stripping its product pipeline.

- On multiple occasions, when external consultants or experts were hired to provide insights, He would dismiss their advice if it didn't align with his personal views, leading to missed opportunities and wasted resources.

- He began to surround himself with a close-knit group of "yes men," effectively isolating himself from any criticism or feedback that could have helped him or the company grow.

- He started promoting employees not based on merit but on personal loyalty to him. This created a culture where sycophancy thrived, and the company's best interests took a back seat.

For five years, Alex's advisors had been sounding the alarm bells. They noticed the cracks in the foundation and saw Benjamin as a liability. They urged Alex to step in, remove Benjamin, and temporarily take over the day-to-day operations until he found a replacement.

But Alex was torn between loyalty to an old friend's son and the unsettling reality that Benjamin's leadership was hurting the company.

His reluctance was also rooted in the vice of Fear—the worry that the company would suffer more if Benjamin left the day-to-day operations and took customers and other stakeholder relationships with him.

But as the days rolled into months and then years, the adverse effects of Benjamin's leadership became too blatant to ignore. Key leaders from various departments started resigning. The final straw was when Helena, a linchpin in the operations team and a dedicated employee of over a decade, handed in her resignation.

As we worked with Alex alongside his advisory team, he began to see his predicament through The 3 Wins lens—that nobody can win if the company loses.

And the company was losing with Benjamin at the helm.

By defining the Company Win, Alex could see how Benjamin had become the barrier—not a building block—for the business to succeed. And with that clarity, Alex became emboldened to finally make the decision he had put off for far too long.

That move launched a dramatic turnaround for the business.

The Company Win Defined

What is the Company Win?

It's about nurturing "the golden goose"—to strengthen your company's short- and long-term growth and marketability prospects.

Your business isn't a lifeless entity driven solely by spreadsheets and financial statements. It's a living organism comprised of people—shareholders, key leaders, rank-and-file employees, contractors, suppliers, customers, and investors—everyone who has a stake in the company's success.

Without a clear definition for your Company Win—based on a Courageous Vision, sound numbers, and talented people—your business will struggle to support your dreams, as you've defined in the Shareholder Win discussed in the previous chapter.

There are four parts to the Company Win:

- Financial Goal-Setting and Review

- Investment and Risk Management

- Key-Leader Development

- Key-Leader Retention

How do you define the Company Win for *your* business?

Part 1: Financial Goal-Setting and Review

The starting point is to set your company's financial targets and give all appropriate stakeholders a clear Line of Sight into how the company is performing relative to those goals.

The idea here is to develop a systematic approach to defining, outlining, and monitoring financial targets and metrics within your business. This process aids in guiding financial decision-making, allocating resources effectively, and strengthening your company's overall financial health and longevity.

What does this process look like?

Consider Amanda:

Amanda runs a company specializing in household water purification systems, generating $5 million in annual revenue. Recognizing a surge in demand as more households prioritize clean water, Amanda envisions significant growth for her business.

Here's what her Courageous Vision might look like when defining her Company Win:

Five-Year Vision: "We will be the top choice for water purification across the country, achieving $30 million in annual revenue while driving health and environmental standards."

Goal Identification: To realize her vision, Amanda sets intermediate financial objectives: annual growth targets, customer acquisition costs, and net profit margins to guide her year-to-year operations. These might include:

- Realize an average of 40% yearly growth in revenue.
- Diversify the product range to cater to varied household needs.
- Partner with leading home appliance retailers.
- Launch educational campaigns about the impact of water quality on health.

Strategy Formulation:

- Invest in R&D for product diversification.
- Pursue both online and offline marketing, targeting health-conscious demographics.

- Showcase products at home and garden trade shows to foster retail partnerships.

- Align with environmental non-governmental organizations (NGOs) for collaborative campaigns.

Financial Growth Modeling: Amanda collaborates with her finance team to create a financial growth model. This model projects the company's EBIT (Earnings Before Interest and Taxes) performance over the next five years, considering market trends, expansion strategies, and operational costs. This way, Amanda can ensure her vision and goals are grounded in reality.

Budgeting: The finance team allocates budgets for R&D, marketing, trade shows, and NGO collaborations while ensuring alignment with the growth model's projections.

Incentive Alignment: Using the growth model, Amanda identifies potential profit milestones. When the company hits these targets, portions are set aside for owner distributions and awards for key leaders. This incentivizes both Amanda and her team to meet and exceed targets. For instance, if the company achieves 45% growth in a particular year, exceeding the projected 40%, a pre-decided bonus percentage would be awarded to Amanda and participating key leaders.

Regular Monitoring (Line of Sight): Amanda introduces monthly financial review meetings. Using dashboards that display real-time data against their projected financial model, the team can promptly identify any deviations and act accordingly.

Analysis: At the end of each quarter, Amanda, along with her finance team, dives deep into the numbers. They evaluate what strategies are working and which ones need rethinking.

For example, they might notice that the countertop units are seeing high sales after a year, but the whole-house systems are below target. And NGO collaborations are generating positive brand resonance.

How does this analysis impact the team's strategy moving forward?

That's where the "Review & Revision" comes in.

Review & Revision: Amanda reallocates some R&D funds to enhance whole-house systems, boosts the budget for NGO partnerships, and introduces financing options to stimulate sales.

Feedback Loop & Stakeholder Visibility: In subsequent reviews, Amanda discusses performance metrics, revised strategies, and potential bonus pools if the stakeholders outperform their targets. She also organizes an annual presentation for shareholders and key partners, highlighting progress towards the 5-year vision and the effectiveness of the incentive alignment.

When everyone aligns toward a shared vision, you'll start seeing a culture of collaboration, motivation, and collective pride, boosting productivity and profit.

Part 2: Investment and Risk Management

Once you've set your financial targets, how do you most effectively manage the company's assets to reach those goals?

This is where investment and risk management comes in, where you allocate and oversee the company's capital resources to achieve specific financial objectives, maximize returns, reduce risks, and ensure sustainable growth.

When founders get this part right with the Company Win, what does that look like?

Consider Lawrence and Jamie, Co-Founders:

The healthcare technology company began as a small startup with a team of 10 but quickly scaled to 125 employees within five years with annual revenues of $50 million.

With profitability climbing, Lawrence and Jamie recognize the importance of effective asset allocation to sustain growth, manage risks, and ensure liquidity. Here's how they might approach achieving their objectives:

Cash Reserves: They maintain a cash balance of $5 million, ensuring they have enough on hand for operational expenses, employee salaries, and short-term unforeseen costs. This allows them to manage day-to-day operations without financial hiccups.

Fixed Assets: Recognizing the importance of technological infrastructure, they allocate $8 million over three years for server upgrades, new workstations, and software licenses, ensuring their product development remains top-notch. They set aside an additional $2 million for acquiring new office space to accommodate their growing team.

Marketable Securities: To maximize returns while ensuring liquidity, they invest $3 million in short-term marketable securities with a diversified mix of treasury bills, blue-chip stocks, dividend-paying stocks, Exchange-Traded Funds (ETFs), and small-cap stocks. These can be quickly liquidated if necessary, balancing growth and liquidity. They made this decision based on the company goals, objectives, time horizon, and risk tolerance. (Disclaimer: Each company will have different needs and objectives.)

Reinvestment into Research and Development (R&D): Believing in continuous innovation, they consistently allocate 15% of their annual profits (which come out to approximately $7.5 million based on the $50 million revenue and assumed margins) into research and development.

Debt Management: They keep a close eye on their debt-to-equity ratio. While they aren't debt-averse, believing in leveraging debt for strategic expansion, they always ensure they aren't overly leveraged. As a result, they've earmarked $2 million annually for servicing any debts and ensuring they are in a comfortable position to either refinance or pay down debts as they mature.

Emergency Fund: On top of their operational cash reserves, Lawrence and Jamie believe in the prudence of having an emergency fund. They set aside $3 million in a high-yield savings account. This acts as a cushion against unforeseen business disruptions or sudden market downturns.

Buy-Sell Agreements with Life Insurance: Lawrence and Jamie have entered into a buy-sell agreement funded with life insurance to ensure business continuity in case either of them passes away or decides to exit. This ensures a clear plan for company ownership and provides funds to execute the agreement. For example, suppose their buy-sell agreement was funded with buy-sell life insurance, and Jamie is killed in a plane crash. Now, Lawrence has the cash from the death benefit to buy out Jamie's spouse without borrowing the funds, using corporate cash, or using an installment sale with Jamie's spouse.

Key Person Insurance: The lead developer, Sarah, is instrumental in the company's software design. A key person insurance policy has been taken out on Sarah to protect against potential financial losses if she passes away. Owners often have critical positions of leadership in the company. Although succession planning is vital, there are always costs associated with the transition of key people, especially in the event of death.

Strategic Alignment: Seeing a growing demand for telemedicine due to global trends, they have allocated $7 million over two years to develop software catering to this niche, anticipating it could open a new revenue stream of $20 million annually.

What would be the results of their investment and risk management strategy, say, two years later? Here are some possible outcomes:

- The company's initial $3 million investments in equities and T-Bills achieve a modest average annual compounded return while remaining liquid and available for long-term strategic initiatives.

- Their R&D investments led to the successful launch of their telemedicine software, which alone has contributed an additional $18 million in its debut year.

- The key person insurance on Sarah, the lead developer, proved pivotal when she faced a health crisis and passed away. The insurance payout helped with the search and recruitment effort that filled her role with two experienced developers, limiting the impact on the product timeline.

- Lawrence and Jamie's buy-sell agreement, funded by life insurance, provides a clear path forward when Jamie dies in the plane crash. Lawrence uses the death benefit to make Jamie's estate (spouse) whole and keeps the cash on hand available for future initiatives. There was also a key-person life insurance policy on Jamie that Lawrence used to recruit a new leader to his position.

By maintaining a diversified asset allocation strategy, the company is safeguarding its present operations and fueling future growth.

Part 3: Key-Leader Development

How do you develop leaders who will help you increase the company's value?

Key-leader development refers to the strategic process of identifying, nurturing, and enhancing the skills and capabilities you deem crucial to your company's current and future success. This involves targeted training, mentorship, exposure to varied experiences, and growth opportunities, ensuring that these leaders can steer the business toward its objectives and sustain its growth.

What does it look like when a founder *doesn't* invest in developing their key leaders?

Consider Tom:

Tom owns a high-growth e-commerce platform company. Despite its initial success and growth, the company is fraught with issues that stem from Tom's lack of investment in his leadership team.

Micromanagement: Tom feels the need to oversee and approve every decision. This stifles the autonomy of his leaders, leading to frustration and a lack of ownership on their part.

Lack of Training: Tom believes in "learning on the job" and doesn't see the need for specialized leadership training or workshops. As a result, his leaders often feel ill-equipped to handle the challenges they face.

Poor Communication: Tom doesn't maintain regular communication with his leadership team. They often feel disconnected from the company's strategic direction and big-picture goals.

Neglecting Feedback: While Tom might occasionally gather feedback, he doesn't act on it or provide a platform where his leaders feel comfortable sharing their concerns or ideas.

No Succession Planning: Tom hasn't considered the company's future beyond his current team. There's no plan for potential turnover or leadership transition, leaving the company vulnerable.

Limited Growth Opportunities: Without mentorship programs, career growth paths, or leadership development initiatives, the leaders feel stagnant in their roles, leading to decreased motivation.

Favoritism: Tom has a few leaders he consistently turns to, sidelining others. This creates a divisive environment and breeds resentment among the leadership team.

What can Tom expect to see if he doesn't change his approach?

High Turnover: Frustrated with the lack of support and growth opportunities, several key leaders leave the company, leading to operational interruptions and the cost of hiring and training replacements.

Reduced Morale: The remaining leaders, seeing their colleagues depart and facing continued neglect, feel demotivated and less invested in the company's success.

Strategic Misalignment: Without regular communication and alignment sessions, different departments start working in silos, leading to inefficiencies and inconsistent customer experiences.

Stagnation: Without innovation and fresh ideas from a motivated leadership team, the company falls behind its competitors, losing market share.

Unlike Tom, successful founders recognize that their leadership team is their most valuable asset. They invest in their growth, empower them with autonomy, communicate openly, and actively seek feedback. By nurturing their leaders, successful business owners foster a culture of innovation, collaboration, and loyalty, driving the long-term success of their business.

Part 4: Key-Leader Retention

You defined what it means to develop your leaders in Part 3 of the Company Win. Now, how do you keep those valuable leaders onboard? How can you improve the odds they won't defect to your competitors or become a competitor themselves?

Consider Leonard:

Leonard is the CEO of a five-year-old Customer Relationship Management (CRM) software company with 50 employees and $5 million in annual revenue. Leonard's key leaders include:

- Mia, the lead software engineer
- Omar, the client relationship manager
- Elise, the product manager.

Let's examine two scenarios. The first scenario is what it might look like if Leonard neglects key-leader retention. The second reflects the adjustments Leonard could make to keep his top talent from leaving.

Scenario 1:

As the company gains market traction, Leonard focuses on attracting bigger clients. While he spends more and more of his time attending tech conferences and networking events to land the "whale" accounts, his team feels neglected.

He assumes the company's growth and momentum would be enough to keep his key leaders motivated and committed.

But Mia feels that her innovative ideas are often sidelined. Omar juggles larger clients with no increase in his team size or compensation. And Elise's roadmap for the product's future is frequently altered without her input.

If things don't change soon, what are the likely outcomes?

Talent Drain: A competitor offers Mia a position with better pay and more creative freedom. The cost to hire and train a software engineer of her caliber is approximately $80,000.

Client Loss: Due to Omar's strained capacity and slower responsiveness, two major clients, contributing $600,000 annually, switched to competing software solutions.

Product Stagnation: Without Elise's clear vision, the product's development stalled, causing a delay in the next software release. This leads to a loss of potential sales of $300,000 for the year.

Reputation Damage: Word spreads in the tight-knit tech community about the dissatisfaction of Leonard's key leaders, making it harder to recruit top talent and damaging the company's standing among potential clients.

Total Direct Loss: $900,000 in revenue + $80,000 in hiring costs = $980,000 that year.

This number does not consider the intangible losses like damage to company culture, a further potential decline in client trust, and the potential innovations that might have come from the experienced leaders had they stayed.

How can Leonard keep this nightmare from becoming a reality? What adjustments can he make to keep his team together, collaborating at the highest level? We find the answers in the following scenario.

Scenario 2:

Recognizing that his key leaders' value far outweighs the retention costs, Leonard prioritizes their well-being and satisfaction. Here are some of the adjustments he makes:

Regular Check-ins and Feedback Sessions: Leonard realizes that continuous communication is essential. He sets up monthly one-on-one meetings with Mia, Omar, and Elise. These sessions allow him to gain insights into their concerns, aspirations, and suggestions, making them feel heard and integral to OmegaTech's vision.

Empowerment and Autonomy: Leonard grants his key leaders the autonomy to make decisions in their respective areas. By trusting Mia with the software's direction, Omar with client relationships, and Elise with product management, they feel a stronger sense of ownership and dedication to the company.

Compensation and Benefits: Realizing the competitive nature of the tech world and the importance of his key leaders, Leonard revises their compensation packages.

- Mia gets a 20% salary increase and is granted stock options worth $100,000, vesting over three years.

- Omar receives a 15% pay raise and a performance bonus linked to client retention and acquisition, with a potential annual bonus of up to $50,000.

- Elise is given a 10% raise and profit-sharing in the product line she oversees, which could translate to an additional $40,000 annually based on current projections.

Long-Term Incentive Plan (LTIP): Besides their new compensation packages, Leonard introduces a long-term incentive plan, allowing his key leaders to participate in the success they help create for the company. If the company achieves an annual profit growth of at least 10% year-on-year for three consecutive years, the key leaders will share another bonus pool of $300,000 at the end of the three years. The bonus pool will be distributed based on their roles and contributions:

- Mia (Lead Software Engineer): $120,000

- Omar Omar (Client Relationship Manager): $90,000

- Elise (Product Manager): $90,000.

Personal Development and Growth: This goes back to Part 3 of the Key-Leader Win. Leonard invests in training programs and courses for his key leaders. He sends Mia to a renowned tech conference, sponsors Omar for a client relationship management course, and enrolls Elise in a leadership workshop.

Recognizing Achievements: Leonard starts publicly acknowledging his team's accomplishments during company-wide meetings, ensuring they receive the recognition they deserve.

What's the impact of these adjustments?

Talent Retention: By retaining Mia, the company avoids the $80,000 recruitment and training costs.

Client Retention and Growth: With Omar's enhanced focus and compensation linked to performance, client retention improves by 5%, leading to an additional $250,000 in annual revenue. Furthermore, he secured three new significant clients, adding another $400,000 in sales.

Product Innovation: Under Elise's motivated leadership, the team launched two new features, bringing in an additional $200,000 in sales.

Improved Reputation: Positive feedback from Mia, Omar, and Elise filters through the tech community, enhancing the company's reputation and attracting more top talent without hefty recruitment fees.

Total Direct Benefit: The company saves $80,000 in recruitment costs and gains an additional $850,000 in revenue, summing up to a positive impact of $930,000 for that year.

Leonard's revamped approach fosters an environment where key leaders are motivated to grow the company. By ensuring they share in the success—both financially and through recognition—Leonard not only retains his star players but also propels the company to new heights.

Beware of Imbalance

Remember, if the Company Win gets out of balance, all stakeholders—including you—will lose.

Consider Mark:

Mark started his business to connect rural areas with fast internet. He set ambitious growth targets as part of his Company Win. But his relentless, hard-driving personality instilled the vice of Busyness among his leadership team, creating a toxic culture that put several employees on the verge of burnout.

At first, the team succeeded rapidly, gaining customer contracts and a growing user base. But over time, there was a noticeable increase in mistakes. Software updates had bugs, systems crashed, and response times lagged.

With a focus solely on activity and hours worked, quality declined. There were no pauses for strategic planning or innovation.

Over time, the frenetic pace began to take its toll. The CTO, Sara, felt the pressure intensely. She worked weekends, leading to strain at home and declining health.

Within a year, she resigned, exhausted, leaving a gap in technical leadership.

Employee turnover soared. New hires would leave within months, citing stress, lack of work-life balance, and an unsupportive environment. The cost of recruiting and training new staff affected the bottom line.

In the unbalanced pursuit of the Company Win, everyone was losing. The key leaders felt underappreciated and burned out. The company was getting a reputation for poor product quality and high employee turnover, as existing clients reconsidered contracts due to unstable service. As the "golden goose" got sick, Mark's dream—his Shareholder Win—began to fray.

So, how could Mark counteract the culture of Busyness he had inadvertently built?

By practicing The Great 8 virtue of Empathy in these ways:

- **Active listening:** Understand team members' concerns, pain points, and ideas. Leaders should have regular one-on-ones where employees feel heard.

- **Work-life balance:** Emphasize the importance of personal time. Encourage vacations and regular breaks.

- **Regular reviews:** Instead of just setting targets, assess whether they are realistic and understand the resources needed. This involves understanding human limitations and the cost of burnout.

- **Professional development**: Invest in training that promotes emotional intelligence, stress management, and effective leadership.

- **Recognize and reward:** Instead of rewarding mere busyness, acknowledge efficiency, innovation, and teamwork.

The Bottom Line

Balancing ambition with The Great 8 Virtues, like Empathy, ensures sustainable success. It preserves the health of the "goose"—the Company Win—which, in turn, produces a steady supply of "golden eggs" to support the Shareholder and Key-Leader wins.

The Next Steps

Here are the immediate steps you can take this week to begin the process of defining your Company Win:

1. Set.

Refer back to the Shareholder Win you defined in the previous chapter. Now, brainstorm on paper: *What does the company need to accomplish for you to achieve your "Win"?* Take your best shot at estimating those company goals.

2. Forecast.

Then, consult with your financial advisory team to help you "sanity check" your assumptions by building a growth model to forecast various scenarios. This way, you and your team can make sound decisions around refining your company's financial goals—and your strategies for hitting those targets.

3. Identify.

Alex's story at the beginning of this chapter teaches us that you and the company can't "Win" without the right leaders on board. Take 30 minutes this week to identify: Which leaders on your team do you need to develop and retain to take your business to the next level? Which leadership roles must you still fill to achieve the Company Win?

CHAPTER 15:
THE KEY-LEADER WIN: INCENTIVIZING (AND SHARING) SUCCESS

"You don't build a business, you build people, then people build the business."
- Zig Ziglar

B y all accounts, Jennifer was a star corporate attorney. She landed big clients, produced exceptional results for them, and garnered a lot of respect from her peers.

But her firm's growth hit a wall.

Despite having a leadership team in place, Jennifer was still the bottleneck. She was the primary source of the firm's most lucrative contracts, while her team showed little initiative in business development. They relied heavily on her reputation and connections, expecting Jennifer to continue being the rainmaker.

Instead of freeing her up, the team deepened the firm's dependency on Jennifer, putting her on the fast track to burnout if things didn't change soon.

That was the scene when we first met with Jennifer a few years ago. She wanted to incentivize her executives to collaborate at a higher level—and share the business development responsibilities, among other things.

But as she looked at her firm through The 3 Wins lens, she realized that most of her leaders weren't the *key* leaders she needed to achieve her vision.

And no amount of incentives would fix that issue.

Identifying *Key* Leaders

We worked with Jennifer on developing criteria for deciding who to keep on her team, who to recruit, and who to incentivize.

Then, we helped her design a long-term incentive plan (LTIP) to reward the behaviors and outcomes she wanted to see more of from her executives.

As she upgraded her team and implemented the LTIP, Jennifer felt the pressure ease. Today, she's no longer the chokepoint because she shares the load with talented leaders with a stake in the firm's success.

How do you identify the key leaders worth recruiting, retaining, and incentivizing?

Everyone's situation is different, as was Jennifer's. But as a general rule of thumb, here are five points to consider:

1. Would the company suffer if they left?

- **Operational Impact:** How would day-to-day operations be affected if this person were to leave suddenly?

- **Relationship Impact:** Does this individual manage key client relationships? If so, would any clients consider leaving with them? How would this person's departure affect relationships with partners, suppliers, or other stakeholders?

- **Team Impact:** What would be the impact on team morale if this individual were to leave? Are there team members who might consider leaving if this person were no longer with the company?

- **Financial Impact:** Would their departure lead to any immediate financial setbacks, like loss of contracts or increased costs? How much would it cost the company in terms of recruitment, training, and lost productivity to replace them?

- **Strategic Impact:** Is this person involved in long-term strategic projects or initiatives? How would their departure affect the trajectory of these projects?

2. Are they collaborative?

Look for key leaders who collaborate with other leaders. This means they can communicate effectively and understand the broader implications of decisions. Their ability to break down silos and foster a cohesive leadership front is crucial to the company's overall success.

3. Do they have an owner's mindset?

Key leaders are owner-minded in their approach to serving and leading others. This means they think and act in ways that benefit the company's long-term health and success. They consider the bigger picture rather than just their department or immediate role. This approach ensures they make decisions that are in the best interest of the company's sustainability and growth.

4. Do they desire to grow the company's profitability and value?

Key leaders take the initiative to improve efficiencies, pursue strategic partnerships, and seize new market opportunities. They understand that profitability isn't just about increasing revenues but also about managing expenses, risks, and resources effectively.

5. Do they bring a "virtuous" decision-making process to the company?

These leaders prioritize doing the right thing over short-term gains, ensuring that the company's reputation, culture, and relationships remain intact and robust. They instill trust within and with external stakeholders, creating a foundation for sustainable success.

Once you've identified your key leaders, it's time to start thinking about the Key-Leader Win.

The Key-Leader Win Defined

What is the Key-Leader Win?

It's about creating an environment where your leaders feel fulfilled in their career path and confident they can build a financial legacy for their families.

When you help your leaders achieve their professional and financial goals, they will have a stronger incentive to perform at their best, contributing to the Company Win—and, ultimately, your Shareholder Win.

There are four parts to the Key-Leader Win:

- Financial Independence
- Leadership Skills Development
- Competitive Base Compensation and Benefits
- Growth Participation

So, how do you define the Key-Leader Win for your business?

Part 1: Financial Independence

In Chapter 13, we discussed *your* financial independence as the first part of the Shareholder Win.

Now, consider your leaders. Does working for you improve their path to hitting their financial independence "number"— the amount they would need to sustain their lifestyle and charitable giving goals without depending on a paycheck?

You can't control whether they ultimately achieve financial independence. But you can give them the tools to help put them on that path.

Consider Colleen and Angela:

Colleen owns a public relations agency with $20 million in annual revenues and 60 employees. Angela is her chief marketing officer (CMO) who has been with the company for five years.

Let's break down the tools Colleen might provide to set Angela on her path to financial independence:

- **Competitive Salary:** Pay a market-leading salary that reflects the value Angela brings to the company.

- **Bonuses:** Implement performance-based bonuses aligning with company goals and her performance.

- **401(k) Plan with Company Match:** Encourage Angela to save more and effectively boost her annual compensation, accelerating her journey towards financial independence.

- **Non-Qualified Deferred Compensation (NQDC) Plan:** Allow her to defer a portion of her salary and bonuses into a future year, which can be particularly tax-efficient and serve as a retirement or long-term savings strategy.

- **Long-Term Incentive Plan:** Allow Angela to participate in the success she is helping create in the business with annual cash bonuses that are contributed to her deferred compensation account by the company.

- **Health and Wellness Benefits:** Help Angela reduce out-of-pocket health-related expenses with comprehensive health coverage, gym memberships, wellness programs, etc.

- **Disability Insurance:** Protect her income if she becomes disabled.

- **Continuing Education:** Offer tuition reimbursement and support for courses, certifications, or degrees that can enhance her skills and value, leading to higher earning potential.

- **Financial Counseling:** Provide access to financial advisors or planners to help Angela strategize her financial journey.

We'll dig deeper into many of these tools in the following three parts of the Key-Leader Win. But, for now, the important takeaway is this: **When you build a reputation for empowering key leaders towards financial independence, the top executive talent will naturally gravitate towards you—and stay with you for the long haul.**

Part 2: Leadership Skills Development

What investments are you making to increase your team's capabilities and potential for achieving the Company Win?

Consistent professional growth empowers key leaders to succeed in their roles. It also clears a path for them to rise in the organization, take on more responsibilities, and earn higher incomes to support their financial independence goals.

What does it look like when an owner "gets it right" with leadership skills development for their executives?

Consider Robert and Maya:

Robert is the CEO of a $30 million commercial construction company that builds office complexes, retail spaces, and industrial facilities. Maya is the chief operating officer (COO) who oversees the full range of operations, from logistics and procurement to site management and quality assurance.

Sensing the industry's rapid evolution and the importance of Maya's role in navigating these changes, Robert believes elevating Maya's leadership skills is essential for the company's continued success.

Here are some professional growth opportunities Robert might provide:

Executive Leadership Program: Robert enrolls Maya in a top-tier executive leadership program, focusing on advanced strategy, organizational dynamics, and global business trends, ensuring she can lead at the highest level in the construction sector.

Supply Chain Optimization Workshop: Given the complexities of construction logistics, Maya attends a workshop centered on leveraging technology and analytics to streamline and optimize the supply chain, ensuring cost savings and efficiency.

Operational Excellence Retreat: Robert sends Maya on a week-long retreat dedicated to achieving operational excellence in construction, focusing on process improvement, lean methodologies, and team alignment.

Mentorship with an Industry Mentor: Robert introduces Maya to a retired industry leader who has successfully run multinational construction firms. This mentorship gives Maya insights, strategies, and a broader understanding of global construction trends.

Executive Coaching: Understanding the unique challenges and pressures of a COO role, Robert hires a seasoned executive coach for Maya. With vast experience in the construction domain, this coach helps her hone leadership skills, manage stress, and balance her executive responsibilities more effectively.

By investing in Maya's development, Robert ensures the company isn't just maintaining its operational efficiency but is also emerging as a market leader. With her elevated skills, Maya becomes an integral figure in shaping the company's future, achieving personal and professional "wins" in the process.

Part 3: Competitive Base Compensation and Benefits

Do your key leaders feel your respect? And by "respect," we mean being well compensated for their work.

While money isn't everything, it's still a significant consideration for your key leaders because it communicates that you value them. How do you develop a competitive base compensation package that shows key leaders the respect they deserve while staying in balance with the company's financial goals?

Consider Emily and Jordan:

Emily owns an IT consulting firm with an annual revenue of $9 million and 37 employees. Here's what her approach might look like when devising a base compensation and benefits package for Jordan, her chief technology officer (CTO).

1. **Base Salary:** Emily's research indicates an average CTO salary of $260,000 for comparable IT firms in her region. Deciding to remain competitive, Emily offers Jordan $275,000.

2. **Performance Bonus:** After consulting with her CFO, Emily determines that a 15% bonus ($41,250) based on company-wide goals could be sustainable, using past performance metrics and industry standards as a guide.

3. **Health Benefits:** Feedback and market quotes lead Emily to a comprehensive group health plan, estimated to cost the company about $5,000 annually per leader.

4. **Retirement Plan:** Emily offers a 401(k) match of 50% up to the first 6% of Jordan's contribution, potentially an extra $8,250 for Jordan.

5. **Continuing Education and Professional Development:** Recognizing the rapid technological changes, Emily allocates $3,000 annually for Jordan's ongoing professional growth.

Jordan's total potential base compensation is $332,500, excluding any opportunities to participate financially in the company's growth, which we'll discuss next in Part 4 of the Key-Leader Win.

While it may seem counterintuitive, generous compensation actually saves money in the long run by attracting better talent, reducing turnover, and driving higher performance.

Part 4: Growth Participation

If you want to build an owner mentality among your leaders, treat them like owners. Allow them to participate in the profit and valuation growth they help create for the company.

How?

In addition to a competitive base compensation package, offer them performance-based incentives such as:

Stock Options or Equity: Award options or shares in the company based on attained benchmarks. This gives key leaders a direct stake in the company's future and can be a powerful retention tool.

Non-Qualified Deferred Compensation (NQDC) Plans: Offer employees the chance to set aside a portion of their salary, bonus, or commission above and beyond their 401k deferral.

Long-Term Incentive Plans (LTIPs): Offer key employees financial rewards over a longer term when specific business goals related to company growth or profitability are achieved. LTIPs are most often used for cash bonuses that the company contributes into the deferred compensation plan.

Employee Stock Ownership Plan (ESOP): Allow employees to become beneficial owners of the stock in their company. Over time, as the company's value grows, so does the stock value held within the ESOP.

Phantom Stock: Provide leaders with the benefits of stock ownership without the company actually giving them any shares. The value of the phantom stock follows the company's actual stock and can be cashed out at specified times or under certain conditions.

Restricted Stock Units (RSUs): RSUs represent a promise to pay a certain number of shares or the cash value of those shares at a future date. Unlike stock options, they also don't require employees to spend money to realize the benefit. As the company's valuation grows, so does the potential payout from RSUs.

In addition to these incentives, companies can formulate various bespoke arrangements based on their specific needs and circumstances. The overarching theme is to create a structure where your key leader's interests align with the company's growth, ensuring mutual benefit and prosperity.

Flexible and Customizable Incentives

For example, one incentive configuration an owner might use is a Non-Qualified Deferred Compensation (NQDC) plan as part of a comprehensive long-term incentive strategy.

Why?

Here are some factors to consider:

- **Alignment with Corporate Goals:** An LTIP's primary objective is to align the interests of executives with the company's long-term objectives. By deferring a portion of compensation until the realization of specified corporate or individual performance benchmarks, the NQDC can encourage sustained performance and loyalty.

- **Tax Efficiency:** NQDCs offer participants an opportunity to defer taxation until funds are distributed in the future. This can be advantageous if the executive believes they will be in a lower tax bracket upon distribution or simply wishes to spread out the tax liability.

- **Flexibility in Design:** Unlike qualified plans, NQDC plans are not bound by many ERISA limits and requirements. This flexibility allows companies to design LTIPs tailored to specific corporate goals or individual performance metrics.

- **Vesting Schedules:** NQDCs within an LTIP can have vesting schedules to further incentivize long-term commitment and performance. This means that while the compensation might be earned in a given year, it might not be fully "owned" by the executive until a set period has elapsed or certain conditions are met.

- **Payout Triggers:** The payout of the deferred amounts in an NQDC can be set to coincide with certain long-term events, such as reaching specific corporate milestones, retirement, or a change in company control.

Remember, flexibility is a good thing. But it also brings a lot of complexities to these types of plans. So, work closely with your financial advisory team with expertise in designing NQDCs and LTIPs. An attorney should review all NQDCs to ensure your plans' compliance with Section 409A of the Internal Revenue Code, which contains strict rules about deferral elections, distributions, and changes to the timing of distributions for NQDCs.

Also, remember that a plan's success hinges on the company's financial health. If the company doesn't hit its benchmarks, it doesn't pay out the awards. Whichever way you design a long-term incentive and retention plan, set it up to "pay for itself" out of the excess profits and valuation growth it creates.

Beware of Imbalance

Now, promoting the Key-Leader Win is a great thing. But, it must also align with the Shareholder and Company wins. Otherwise, you can expect the vice of Territorialism to creep in, where certain leaders pursue "winning" at others' expense.

Consider Jim, Peter, and Heather:

Jim owns a transportation firm that earns $8 million in annual revenues with 32 employees. In recent years, Jim implemented a long-term incentive plan (LTIP) to reward and retain his key leaders for their participation in the company's success.

But Peter, his vice president of sales, isn't happy with the plan. He resents that Heather, vice president of human resources, receives a share of the award.

"Why should Heather get the same benefit as me?" Peter complains. "I'm the one out there bringing in the revenue. The award pool gets diluted with her included."

His resentment leaks into strategic meetings where Peter becomes less cooperative with Heather, often questioning her contributions and belittling the HR department's role.

You can imagine how this situation unfolds. Peter feels entitled to a larger award because he perceives the sales department as the primary revenue generator and, hence, more deserving than Heather.

As a result, Heather and her team become less inclined to support Peter and his sales initiatives, fearing their efforts will be unappreciated or belittled.

Unfortunately, Peter doesn't understand that, with the way Jim designed the plan, Peter could earn a much larger reward from the LTIP if he works with Heather and not against her.

So, how could Jim counteract the vice of Territorialism infecting his leadership team?

By demonstrating The Great 8 virtue of Peacemaking in these ways:

- **Opening the dialogue:** Initiate a conversation between Peter and Heather to address the issue. Let both parties express their feelings and concerns.

- **Highlighting the value:** Explain that every department plays a crucial role. While sales might bring revenue, HR ensures the company attracts, retains, and nurtures the talent that makes such revenue possible.

- **Reinforcing the purpose:** Clarify the purpose of the LTIP. It's not just about the direct award but also the company's long-term growth and sustainability.

- **Encouraging collaboration:** Initiate joint projects or team-building exercises for the sales and HR teams, fostering collaboration and mutual respect.

What if Peter refuses to back down?

If all interventions fail, Jim may need to consider whether Peter, despite his sales prowess, is the right fit for the company's culture and long-term vision.

Ultimately, all stakeholders must recognize that the company's success is a collective effort. While revenue generation is essential, the roles supporting and sustaining revenue, like HR, are equally crucial.

The Bottom Line

As Starbucks founder Howard Schultz said, "Success is best when it's shared."

Sharing success cultivates a sense of ownership and pride among the leadership team. It fosters a collaborative environment where leaders understand that their individual success is inextricably linked to the success of their colleagues and the business as a whole.

The Next Steps

Here are the immediate steps you can take this week to begin the process of defining the Key-Leader Win:

1. Assess.

Brainstorm on paper with prompts like these:

- "Do we have the right leaders in the right roles?"
- "What leadership roles do we still need to fill?"
- "Where are the weak points?"

- "What adjustments do we need to make to strengthen our team and improve collaboration?"

2. Align.

Schedule time with your financial advisory team to review your existing incentive plans. Do the incentives align with the interests of all stakeholders? Are they working to retain your key leaders and promote the behaviors you want? What changes should you make? Should you add any new incentives?

3. Observe.

Be intentional about getting your finger on the pulse of your leadership team. Do they collaborate well? Do they respect each other? Do they appear happy with their work? If you see anything that's off, spend some time with those leaders to get their feedback and discuss ways you can help them "win."

PART 4:
UNLEASH THE COLLABORATION EFFECT ON PROFIT

CHAPTER 16:
PUTTING IT ALL TOGETHER: UNLEASHING THE CEOP IN YOUR BUSINESS—AND YOUR LIFE

"If everyone is moving forward together, then success takes care of itself."

- Henry Ford

This is the book's final chapter, but we intend it to be the start of your transformation story.

Think of this chapter as an ancient treasure map guiding you to the founder's "holy grail"—the Collaboration Effect on Profit (CEOP). **Once you've discovered and unleashed the CEOP, you will begin tasting that elusive freedom you've sought since you launched your entrepreneurial journey.**

While the path to the CEOP is fraught with obstacles and pitfalls, this book has revealed the tools you need to navigate those challenges and succeed. So far, you've learned how to:

1. Fight off Founder's Syndrome by strengthening your **character** through The Great 8 Virtues.

2. Transform your **culture** by instilling The Great 8 Virtues throughout the company.

3. Boost **financial performance** by defining and balancing The 3 Wins.

But how do you put it all together as you embark on your journey? How do you align these concepts of character, culture, and financial performance to grab hold of the "holy grail" and unleash its power in your business and life? Follow these six steps.

Step 1: Diagnose

Identify your most prominent vulnerabilities to Founder's Syndrome.

Founder's Syndrome is where the founder maintains excessive control and influence over the organization, often to its detriment. Founder's Syndrome arises when your desire for control outweighs your openness to collaboration. Too much control stifles collaboration and chokes off growth.

At the root of Founder's Syndrome are these eight universal vices impacting every founder to varying degrees.

Vice #1: Egotism

Egotism is "the excessive practice of thinking and talking about oneself due to an inflated sense of self-worth." Unchecked, Egotism hinders your ability to trust and empower your team, stifles ambitious thinking, and discourages hiring talented individuals to bring your dreams to life.

Vice #2: Busyness

Busyness is not the same as "being busy." But when your work consumes you, "busy" crosses the line to a vice that strains your relationships, diminishes productivity, and causes team burnout.

Vice #3: Distraction

Distraction is taking your eye off the proverbial ball—your mission, team, and priorities. And that's when you become most prone to making costly mistakes. You divert your attention from important tasks and goals to engage in trivial or sometimes harmful activities, undermining your productivity, relationships, and personal development.

Vice #4: Greed

Greed is the selfish pursuit of money, pleasure, and power at the expense of others' interests. These pursuits are not inherently wrong, but when approached with improper motives, they become destructive, leaving you unsatisfied and empty.

Vice #5: Anger

Anger arises when obstacles prevent you from achieving your desires. Although occasional expressions of anger are justified (as in "righteous indignation"), uncontrolled Anger is harmful. It deteriorates trust, hampers team performance, and may push your most talented employees to seek opportunities elsewhere.

Vice #6: Dishonesty

Dishonesty involves intentionally lying or withholding truth for personal gain or self-preservation. Such deception can lead to the breakdown of trust and fairness in relationships. When Dishonesty influences your decisions, you become divided, living a double life: one aligned with truth and the other struggling to reconcile truth with your actions.

Vice #7: Territorialism

Territorialism embodies a "Reverse Golden Rule" mindset: *Do unto others before they do it to you.* It compels you to protect your status, reputation, and turf, regardless of the cost to others. This vice creates a divisive atmosphere, promotes unproductive competition, and encourages a zero-sum mindset.

Vice #8: Fear

Fear is a natural emotion that signals potential threats. However, when Fear becomes excessive or unfounded, it becomes a destructive vice. It narrows your perspective, highlighting only the worst-case scenarios and limiting your ability to consider all options and make well-informed decisions.

Which vices are at the root of your current bout with Founder's Syndrome? **Take the Founder's Syndrome Root Cause Survey in Chapter 2** to identify your most prominent vulnerabilities so you can start counteracting them immediately.

Step 2: Treat

Develop a treatment plan with The Great 8 Virtues.

Dig deeper into The Great 8 Virtues (Chapters 3-10) by answering the "Deeper Reflection" questions at the end of each chapter. This exercise will spur your thinking to develop an effective "treatment plan" to fight off Founder's Syndrome.

In the meantime, here's an overview of the virtues with an example action item for each:

Virtue #1: Humility vs. Egotism (Chapter 3):

Humility leads to self-awareness, the starting point to overcoming Founder's Syndrome.

> **Action:** *Ask yourself, "Am I the bottleneck to our growth? Is what I'm doing working? What do I need to change to improve results?"*

Virtue #2: Empathy vs. Busyness (Chapter 4):

Empathy forces you to slow down your mind. It helps you see what is most important, not only for yourself but also for your people.

> **Action:** *Look for opportunities to reach out to your team and take a genuine interest in their work and lives. Discover what they get excited about and what concerns them the most. Understanding your team's perspective will reveal how you can best set them up for success.*

Virtue #3: Attentiveness vs. Distraction (Chapter 5):

Attentiveness focuses your attention on the goal, makes you more decisive, reduces "boneheaded" mistakes, and keeps you calm under pressure.

> **Action:** *Clarify your vision and mission. When you're unclear on your priorities, you become vulnerable to getting distracted by other people's agendas.*

Virtue #4: Accountability vs. Greed (Chapter 6):

Accountability is giving permission to select people to ask the hard questions. It's about opening yourself up to scrutiny: "Look, if you see me acting in ways that don't reflect our values, let me know."

> **Action:** *Who are the people you trust and respect, and who would be willing to hold you accountable? Seek them out. Spend consistent time with them. Invite them to hold your feet to the fire. Ask for their advice on overcoming the struggles you're confronting.*

Virtue #5: Acceptance vs. Anger (Chapter 7):

Acceptance puts you in a calm and resourceful mental state. You can see the potential in each team member despite their current performance. And you gain insight into where to put them in the company so they can flourish individually and as a team.

> **Action:** *Put yourself in an "accepting" frame of mind. When you notice people underperforming, how can you help them improve? Use this Acceptance Inventory to put you in the right mindset:*

- *Why did I hire them in the first place?*

- *What is causing them to underperform?*

- *What areas of giftedness do they bring to the table?*

- *How do they know when they are "on"–working in their sweet spot?*

- *Are they still a good fit for what we are trying to do?*

- *Are they open to being coached? Will they listen?*

- *What exactly do I want them to do now?*

- *Have I been clear in articulating my expectations?*

These questions will help you see the possibilities in the person and discover the most effective course of action.

Virtue #6: Integrity vs. Dishonesty (Chapter 8):

The English word for Integrity comes from the Latin *integer*, meaning "wholeness, completeness." So, think of Integrity as the virtue of "being whole" based on consistency of character. As serial entrepreneur and angel investor Naval Ravikant defines, "Integrity is when what you think and what you say and what you do are one."

> **Action:** *Get honest with yourself. We're human. We all make poor decisions, including ones where we play fast and loose with the truth. But when you recognize what you've done, come clean, outline a plan to correct the issue, and take action.*

Virtue #7: Peacemaking vs. Territorialism (Chapter 9):

Territorialism is about scarcity–fear of loss. It causes people to get defensive and protect their turf at all costs. It sees business as a zero-sum game: "For me to win, I must make sure you lose." But Peacemaking takes on an abundance mindset. It says, "If you and I can resolve our differences and work together, we both can win–and on a much bigger scale than either of us could achieve alone."

> **Action:** *Invite candid conversations. Peacemakers surround themselves with a "team of rivals" who challenge their thinking. They're not afraid of confrontation or dissenting opinions. Instead, they invite candid conversations. That's because they understand that allowing healthy disagreements creates a high-trust culture where collaboration can flourish.*

Virtue #8: Courage vs. Fear (Chapter 10):

Courage is about being clear-eyed about the dangers that lie ahead but acting anyway. It's an unshakeable conviction that if you fail to act now, you will create an even worse outcome than you feared.

Action: *When you face situations that cause Fear, don't try to sweep that feeling under the rug of optimism. You'll feel discouraged and lose faith. Instead, apply the Stockdale Paradox. Confront the "brutal facts" of the situation— no matter how bad they seem. And with Courage, take immediate and ongoing action to improve your situation.*

Step 3: Instill

Begin instilling The Great 8 Virtues throughout your company.

When working with clients at Legacy, we have a series of eight workshops—one for each Great 8 virtue—focused on instilling that virtue throughout the company.

We touch on the big ideas behind these workshops in each Great 8 chapter (Chapters 3-10). As you review those chapters, look for the sections titled "Humility at Scale" (Chapter 3), "Empathy at Scale" (Chapter 4), "Attentiveness as Scale (Chapter 5), etc.

Our workshop series begins with the last virtue—Courage— because it focuses on setting a Courageous Vision, a natural starting point for building the other workshops around.

Here is a brief overview of the eight workshop topics:

1. Courage at Scale: Set a Courageous Vision (Chapter 10)

Winston Churchill's "Finest Hour" speech offers a powerful framework for helping you set a Courageous Vision for making tough decisions and taking bold action to get through any challenge that threatens your company's growth.

Chapter 10 breaks down Churchill's framework in these five steps:

1. Set a Courageous Vision
2. Provide evidence that supports your conviction
3. Confront the (brutal) facts.
4. Count the cost of inaction.
5. Paint a vivid picture of success.

2. Humility at Scale: Role Optimization (Chapter 3)

Assess your own and your team's performance. Is everyone placed in the best position to achieve professional and personal fulfillment? If not, what adjustments can you make to bridge the gaps between their actual and optimal roles?

We call this exercise "Role Optimization." It taps into Jim Collin's idea in *Good to Great*: Get the right people "on the bus" and then put them in "the right seats"–their optimal role.

The exercise requires self-awareness, open-mindedness, and confidence. In other words, all participants must practice Humility to get it right.

We dig deeper into the Role Optimization process in Chapter 3.

3. Empathy at Scale: Most Important Tasks (Chapter 4)

Defining the Most Important Tasks (MITs) for each role empowers you and your team to create margin–freed up time–to operate with more Empathy and less Busyness. The idea is to identify the two to three most important tasks you must complete each week that make the most significant impact on your company's success.

Example MITs:

- **COO:** "Assess every deliverable or request that my VPs need from me and respond by the end of the day each Friday."

- **Project Manager:** "Review all invoices by seven days before the invoice due date."

- **Sales Rep:** "Make 20 'touches' with new prospects by the end of the day Thursday of each week."

We detail the process for setting MITs in Chapter 4.

4. Attentiveness at Scale: Line of Sight (Chapter 5)

As the owner, you have a clear Line of Sight, but others on the team often get left in the dark. As a result, even the most talented employees won't perform at the level you'd expect.

Why? If team members don't see what they're working towards, how do they know whether they're making progress? They don't have a clear vision to help guide their decisions—what they should say "Yes" or "No" to. So, they get distracted by unproductive tasks, turf wars, and office politics. They take their eye off the ball because they don't know what that "ball" is.

With Line of Sight, employees can focus on helping the company hit its targets. As John Doerr writes in *Measure What Matters*, "Contributors are most engaged when they can see how their work contributes to the company's success. Quarter to quarter, day to day, they look for tangible measures of their achievement."

How do you create an environment that promotes Line of Sight? Establish a productive meeting routine for reviewing progress toward the company's targets.

Patrick Lencioni recommends four types of meetings in *Death by Meeting: A Leadership Fable...About Solving the Most Painful Problem in Business*. Each meeting type has a unique goal, duration, and agenda.

We unpack these four meeting types in Chapter 5 for you and your team to gain a clearer Line of Sight:

1. Daily Check-Ins
2. Weekly Tactical
3. Monthly Strategic
4. Quarterly Off-Site Review.

5. Accountability at Scale: Achievement Updates (Chapter 6)

The big idea is to shift from a traditional performance review model to Achievement Updates.

Why?

After most performance reviews, employees think:

- *What was the point of that review?*
- *Honestly, I still have no idea how I'm doing.*
- *Why not tell me what I did wrong when I can do something to fix it—not several months later?!*

Achievement Updates counteract the shortcomings of traditional performance reviews by providing timely, consistent, and *valuable* feedback between owners, managers, and employees.

Go to Chapter 6 for ideas on implementing Achievement Updates in your company.

6. Acceptance at Scale: Personality and Leadership Style Assessments (Chapter 7)

Tools such as Myers-Briggs, DiSC Profile, and Enneagram can equip you and your team with a shared vocabulary for discussing each other's differences. They offer insights into how to listen and speak to one another based on awareness of each other's strengths and personalities.

But beware of the temptation of using assessment results against people, especially in these two ways:

- **Labeling and limiting them:** "They're an introvert. They wouldn't be good at sales."

- **Patronizing them:** "You're a high S and C, and that's why you don't [fill in the blank]."

Instead, use your understanding of your team's similarities and differences to "accept" who they are (and want to become). This way, you gain a clearer insight into where to put them in the best positions to succeed.

See Chapter 7 to spur ideas on using—and avoiding misusing—assessments with your team.

7. Integrity at Scale: High-Trust Communication (Chapter 8)

High-Trust Communication is about being transparent and candid with others—especially when delivering unpleasant news.

Read Chapter 8 to learn how to model these four steps to High-Trust Communication:

1. Connect with your audience.

2. Speak with candor.

3. Show them respect.

4. Lead them to action or a solution.

8. Peacemaking at Scale: Healthy Conflict Management (Chapter 9)

In *Up the Organization: How to Stop the Corporation from Stifling People and Strangling Profits*, Robert Townsend writes, "A good manager doesn't try to eliminate conflict; he tries to keep it from wasting the energies of his people. If you're the boss and your people fight you openly when they think you are wrong—that's healthy."

Townsend makes an important point: As the boss, stop trying to prevent conflict. Don't push everyone to "be positive" or dismiss dissenters as "negative influences."

Instead, show your team what healthy conflict looks like. Otherwise, people will default to keeping their disagreements to themselves. Instead of eliminating conflict, you will have only suppressed it.

Where do you begin to resolve a tense situation using Healthy Conflict Management? We discuss these four steps to Healthy Conflict Management in detail in Chapter 9:

1. Take the initiative

2. Understand the other person's perspective

3. Confirm your understanding

4. Share your perspective.

Step 4: Define

Define The 3 Wins for you, the company, and your key leaders.

The 3 Wins Framework offers a holistic and balanced approach to financial decision-making. The idea is to align all three wins simultaneously:

- The Shareholder Win

- The Company Win

- The Key-Leader Win.

Otherwise, everyone will ultimately lose if one party wins, but the other two do not.

So, how do you align The 3 Wins? The first step is to define each "win," starting with the Shareholder Win.

The Shareholder Win (Chapter 13)

The Shareholder Win is about getting beyond "survival mode" to build a sustainably profitable business that produces the means you need to build an impactful financial legacy in your family for generations to come.

The five parts to the Shareholder Win:

- **Part 1: Financial independence:** What's your number? How much do you need—apart from your company's value—to sustain your desired lifestyle indefinitely without additional employment income? What's your timeline for reaching that number?

- **Part 2: Ownership transition planning:** What's your plan for ownership transition and succession planning to achieve your financial independence objectives?

- **Part 3: Estate and tax planning:** When you've worked hard to achieve your financial independence goals, how do you prepare to pass on that "win" to the people and causes you care about the most? How do you ensure a smooth transfer of ownership and control of *all* your assets upon retirement, incapacity, or death?

- **Part 4: Family legacy planning:** How can you ensure you can share your "win" with the people and causes you care about the most for future generations, according to your values and pre-set terms?

- **Part 5: Wealth management:** The previous four parts of the Shareholder Win pertain to setting your targets and creating realistic plans for achieving them. But how do you successfully execute those plans? How do you stay on track as market dynamics and risk tolerances fluctuate over time?

The Company Win (Chapter 14)

The Company Win is about nurturing "the golden goose"—to strengthen your company's short- and long-term growth and marketability prospects.

The four parts to the Company Win:

- **Part 1: Financial Goal-Setting & Review:** What are your company's financial targets? Do all appropriate stakeholders have a clear Line of Sight on how the company is performing relative to those goals?

- **Part 2: Investment and Risk Management:** Once you've set your financial targets, how do you most effectively manage the company's assets to reach those goals?

- **Part 3: Key-Leader Development:** How do you develop leaders who will help you increase the company's value? What is your process for identifying, nurturing, and enhancing the skills and capabilities you deem crucial to your company's current and future success?

- **Part 4: Key-Leader Retention:** You defined what it means to develop your leaders in Part 3 of the Company Win, but how do you keep those valuable leaders onboard? How can you improve the odds they won't defect to your competitors or become a competitor themselves?

The Key-Leader Win (Chapter 15)

The Key-Leader Win is about creating an environment where your leaders feel fulfilled in their career path and confident they can build a financial legacy for their families.

The four parts to the Key-Leader Win:

- **Part 1: Financial Independence:** Does working for you improve their path to hitting their financial independence "number"—the amount they would need to sustain their lifestyle and charitable giving goals without depending on a paycheck?

- **Part 2: Leadership Skills Development:** What investments are you making to increase your team's capabilities and potential for achieving the Company Win? Are you offering consistent professional growth opportunities to empower key leaders to succeed in their roles?

- **Part 3: Competitive Base Compensation and Benefits:** Do your key leaders feel your respect? And by "respect," we mean being well compensated for their work. While money isn't everything, it's still a significant consideration for your key leaders because it communicates that you value them.

- **Part 4: Growth Participation:** Are you allowing your leaders to participate in the profit and valuation growth they help create for the company? How do they get to participate—long-term incentive plan, stock options, phantom stock, etc.? After all, if you want to build an owner mentality among your leaders, treat them like owners.

A Caveat

If you're looking at the multiple parts for each Win and thinking, "Whoah! That's a lot of ground to cover," it's okay. You don't have to tackle all parts of The 3 Wins simultaneously. In fact, the entire process of fully fleshing out your 3 Wins strategy may take years.

But the critical point is that you *begin* defining The 3 Wins ASAP. The sooner you get started, the quicker you'll achieve alignment that sets the Collaboration Effect on Profit in motion.

Step 5: Assemble

Build a CEOP advisory team to help you define, align, and consistently execute The 3 Wins.

If you feel overwhelmed with defining The 3 Wins, that's why it's important to build what we call a CEOP advisory team.

This is a comprehensive team of professionals with expertise to support you in the specific aspects of The 3 Wins. Your team might include:

A Certified Financial Planner (CFP):

- Assist in personal financial planning, ensuring financial independence and goal-setting.

- Review and provide guidance on asset management and investment strategies.

A Certified Public Accountant (CPA) or Tax Advisor:

- Provide expertise in tax planning and compliance, helping to optimize tax positions.

- Assist in financial record-keeping and reporting.

An Executive Compensation Consultant:

- Advise on competitive compensation and benefits packages.

An Executive Benefits Advisor:

- Design, implement, and manage profit-sharing plans, long-term incentive plans, non-qualified deferred compensation plans, Employee Stock Ownership Plans, etc.

- Ensure that key leaders are motivated and engaged through participation in the company's profit and valuation growth.

An Investment Advisor:

- Guide business investments, portfolio management, and risk management strategies.

An Insurance Advisor:

- Assist in identifying and mitigating risks through appropriate insurance coverages.

An Estate Planning Attorney:

- Help establish wills, trusts, and other estate planning structures.
- Guide family legacy planning and ensure the smooth transition of assets.

A Family Legacy Advisor:

- Assist in creating a plan to preserve and continue the family's values and wealth across generations.

A Business Attorney:

- Advise on legal structures, contracts, and other legal aspects of business operations.
- Assist in business ownership transition planning.

A Business Valuation Expert:

- Provide business valuation services crucial for ownership transitions and investment decisions.

A Mergers and Acquisitions Advisor:

- Assist in planning and executing business ownership transition, whether a sale, merger, or acquisition.

A Business Coach or Mentor:

- Guide strategic planning, leadership development, and operational improvements.

At Legacy, we often serve as the CEOP Advisory Team Lead, helping our clients assemble their teams with experts who best fit their needs and situations.

But the key here is to start somewhere, with someone. Then, flesh out your CEOP Advisory Team from there. Ask your current advisors for recommendations for experts in roles you need to fill, when you need to fill them.

Step 6: Review

Develop a "Continuous Improvement" process for tracking progress and making adjustments that produce—and perpetuate—the Collaboration Effect on Profit.

By now, you've familiarized yourself with The Great 8 Virtues and The 3 Wins Framework.

You're working on strengthening your character and company culture to fully embrace collaboration.

You've started to assemble your CEOP Advisory Team to help you define, align, and execute The 3 Wins to boost financial performance.

You've taken that first step in the right direction toward producing the CEOP.

But as you progress on your journey, remember that the CEOP is not a set-it-and-forget strategy. Market conditions will change. Your personal and family life will change. Founder's

Syndrome will flair up. Factors outside your control will knock any of The 3 Wins out of alignment.

In fact, producing and perpetuating the CEOP requires consistent attention. That's why we recommend our clients conduct periodic CEOP reviews—at least quarterly. This way, they can make timely adjustments to keep their business on the right trajectory.

The Bottom Line: The CEOP Fuels Your Legacy

When you combine The 3 Wins with The Great 8 Virtues, you create a high-trust, high-performance culture that attracts the most talented people to rally around your vision. You see key leaders and rank-and-file employees all working together in their optimal roles toward the same goal, reaching a level of collaboration that makes your company unstoppable.

In other words, you bring to life Patrick Lencioni's quote, **"If you could get all the people in an organization rowing in the same direction, you could dominate any industry, in any market, against any competition, at any time."**

That's what the Collaboration Effect on Profit looks like. It's the powerful force generated when you align character, culture, and financial performance to win in any market. It's a force for success available to any founder who will relentlessly pursue it. And it's a force that creates the ideal conditions for passing the baton of your business—your legacy—to the next-generation leaders.

Where Do You Go From Here?

David Harper

Now that you've discovered The Great 8 Virtues, The 3 Wins, and the CEOP, what will you do about it? What's your plan of action?

One of the reasons we wrote this book was to institutionalize our process. We've seen firsthand that the principles work. But the CEOP is not a quick fix. It's a long-term path toward achieving *sustainable* success that accrues value for all stakeholders connected to you and your vision.

Sure, there are many methods for making a lot of money. But most of them leave behind such significant collateral damage that it raises the question Jesus asked, "What does it profit a man to gain the whole world and forfeit his soul?"

But we've discovered that **when you set the Collaboration Effect on Profit in motion, you'll achieve a "success"—however you define it—that won't require forfeiting your soul.** It's a success that encourages others to achieve their dreams alongside you. And it's a lasting success—to build a legacy that blesses the people and charitable causes you care about the most for generations to come.

So, what's your starting point? How do you set the CEOP in motion in your business and life?

1. Start now, wherever you are.

Discuss The Great 8 Virtues and The 3 Wins with your team and get their "buy-in."

Ask your key leaders to rank the team's current level of collaboration on a scale of 1-10—one being the lowest and ten, the highest. If they say four or five, what would it take to raise the team's collaboration to an eight, nine, or ten? What would need to change in yourselves and the business to achieve that level?

Once you've sketched out a plan, just get started. Much of what we talk about in this book, you can implement yourself. So, go for it!

If you have specific questions about your situation, feel free to contact us at rclemmer@ legacyadvisorypartners.com. We can talk you through some of those scenarios to get you moving in the right direction. If you need someone to walk alongside you under a more formal engagement, we could do that, too. **But most of all, we just want you to get started— to begin breaking the grip of Founder's Syndrome and tasting the fruits of the CEOP.**

2. Find support.

From what we're seeing, there seems to be a movement of God at work in the marketplace. He's stirring the hearts of entrepreneurs worldwide to create more virtuous companies—to make a positive impact on all the lives their companies touch every day.

So, join a group of like-minded business leaders and encourage each other in your individual and collective pursuits. There are many great organizations you can connect with. At Legacy, we've connected with many friends within Fellowship of Companies for Christ International (https://www.fcci-site.com/), and it has been an amazing journey.

3. Be the change.

Matthew 7:13-14 says, "Enter by the narrow gate; for wide is the gate and broad is the way that leads to destruction, and there are many who go in by it. Because narrow is the gate and difficult is the way which leads to life, and there are few who find it."

There are many disturbing trends in the U.S. and around the world today. Let's call them the "broad way." These trends directly oppose everything we've described in the CEOP—which we'll call the "narrow way."

The "broad way" leads to the exploitation of different groups of people. It's connected to the greedy pursuit of making money at the expense of everything else. And it comes from a scarcity mindset that chooses to create monopolies that limit opportunity instead of an abundance mindset that promotes merit and expands prosperity.

We believe a grassroots campaign around sharing and practicing the principles of the CEOP is an effective way to "be the change" we hope to see in our companies, our families, and the world.

All it takes is one person who engages another, who engages another, and so on down the line to create exponential awareness and change.

Our friend Bobby Mitchell, Jr., with the Fellowship of Christian Companies International (FCCI), has researched the number of business leaders needed in the U.S. to effectively reverse many of the negative, vice-oriented trends we see in companies and the world today.

He said the number is 10,000—if each leader can engage and influence 160 people every year.

Just 10,000 business leaders? 160 people? Now, *that* seems doable! Will you join us to be one of the 10,000?

We hope and pray you will. Let's do this together!

APPENDIX

Scan the QR code to access and download the latest tools and resources to help you unleash the Collaboration Effect on Profit in your company. (Or, go to CollaborationEffectOnProfit.com.)

ABOUT THE AUTHORS

J. David Harper, Jr.

J. David Harper, Jr., is the founder and chairman of **Legacy Advisory Partners**, a financial services and executive benefits firm based in Alpharetta, Georgia. He is also the author of *The Great 8: A New Paradigm for Leadership* (the precursor to this book) and co-author (with his wife, Anne) of *Light Their Fire for God: Seven Powerful Virtues for Kids.*

David not only speaks and writes about the idea of leaving a lasting legacy, but he also lives it. He's actively involved in organizations making a significant global impact, like the Young Life Atlanta Project and Young Life North Africa Middle East. And his roles with the Fellowship of Christian Companies International (FCCI), Heritage Forum, and Legendary Leadership underscore his commitment to promoting faith-based principles to achieve excellence in the markeplace.

At the heart of David's life is his family—his wife, Anne, and their three children, who have blessed them with twelve grandchildren.

David earned a B.A. in English at Davidson College, where he was also the starting quarterback on the football team.

Connect with David at <u>dharper@legacyadvisorypartners.com</u>.

Russell H. Clemmer, IV

Russell H. Clemmer, IV, brings over a decade of experience in business development, consulting, and finance to his role as CEO of **Legacy Advisory Partners**. He holds a B.A. from Columbia International University, an MBA from Gardner-Webb University, and Series 7 and 66 certifications.

Russ is also the host of **The 3 Wins Podcast** (https://the3wins.substack.com/), which delves into topics at the intersection of faith, financial growth, and entrepreneurship.

Outside of the office, Russ enjoys woodworking and spending quality time with his wife, Lauren, and their four children. An active member of First Baptist Church Alpharetta, Russ also serves at the Fellowship of Companies for Christ International (FCCI), an organization committed to aligning faith and business success.

Having grown up working for his father's landscaping company, Russ learned firsthand the value of determination and discipline in entrepreneurship. As Russ puts it, "All work, when done well, is hard. There are obstacles to overcome, challenges to meet, and the vices of life to guard against. Anything worthwhile takes hard work!"

With this grounded perspective, he brings an authentic, relatable voice to the conversation around achieving lasting success in business and life.

Connect with Russ at rclemmer@legacyadvisorypartners.com.

Sean M. Lyden

Sean M. Lyden is CEO of **Lyden Communications, LLC**, an Orlando, Florida-based sales training and media company for founders looking to systematize their sales and scale their business.

He's also the host of the **Systematic Selling Podcast** (https://www.systematicselling.co/), which breaks down the strategies, trends, and best practices that help founders scale their sales and build a business they love.

A business journalist for over two decades, Sean is the co-author of *How to Succeed and Make Money on Your First Rental House* (John Wiley & Sons) and a contributor to *The Ultimate Small Business Marketing Guide* and *The Great Big Book of Business Lists*, both books published by Entrepreneur Press (*Entrepreneur Magazine*).

Sean holds a B.A. in English Literature from Samford University in Birmingham, Alabama, where he was a scholarship athlete in cross country and track. He and his wife, Jennifer, have two grown daughters and one grandson.

Connect with Sean at sean@lydencommunications.com.

DISCLOSURE

Securities offered through Registered Representatives of Cambridge Investment Research, Inc., a broker-dealer, member FINRA/SIPC. Advisory services offered through CIRA, a Registered Investment Adviser. Legacy Advisory Partners and Cambridge are not affiliated. Cambridge does not offer tax or legal advice.